The *Butterfly* WITH TORN WINGS

A MEMOIR OF STAYING ALIVE

GIOVANNA MARIA ACCIAVATTI

ALESSANDRA TAMERIN
CO-WRITER

bookbaby

║\ bookbaby

Cover and interior design by Rose Unes

Illustration (p. 77) by Sue Estrada, reprinted with permission

ISBN: 978-1483570129

Dedication
MY BOOK, MY LIFE, MY LOVE

I dedicate my tears and joy to my Mamma and Papà, who gave back my life to me. I was like a golden drop from the sky, covered with a blanket, where the angels circled all around me.

I also dedicate my book to my baby, the little flower; to my nieces Virginia, Lucia, and Elia; to my nephews, Marco, Tony, and Vinny; and to my Lisa.

Contents

Foreword

In the summer of 2015, a vivacious, diminutive woman tripped lightly into my English class at Westchester Community College, bringing with her an air of both sophistication and playfulness. She was elegantly dressed in a light, summery outfit and high-heeled shoes. The minute she came in, the atmosphere in our class shifted perceptibly. Here was a woman who had lived, and who had a great deal to say about life! Although she wasn't able to come to every class, Giovanna made quite an impression on her fellow students, and we all looked forward to her visits. She told us that she wrote poetry—in English—and she was brave enough to read some of her poems aloud. Later, she confided that she had been working on a memoir about her life, and that the project was proving to be a challenge. When I offered to work with her as her editor, she immediately agreed.

We had already noticed that we share the same first and middle names. As we began working together on her project, I discovered that Giovanna's family was from Abruzzo, the same region in Italy where my mother's family originated. Giovanna was familiar with all the regional recipes that my mother had cooked throughout my childhood! Cooking and food are monumentally important to Italians, and this coincidence strengthened our connection. Not only did Giovanna invite me to her house to work on the book, but she also prepared delicious Italian dishes for me, that brought me back to my own childhood in my mother's kitchen.

Giovanna is a storyteller. Although her story is often painful, Giovanna's spirit and sense of humor are indomitable, and her courage in the face of adversity is truly inspiring.

—*Johanna Maria Rose*

Acknowledgements

My deepest thanks to my teacher and editor, Johanna Maria Rose. Without her patience, encouragement, and expertise, this book would not have been finished.

I am grateful to my young friend and co-writer, Alessandra Tamerin, who always included me in every family event, enjoying happy moments together with her son and her beautiful mamma.

Introduction

Since I was a young girl, and became aware of the immensity of the sea, I have always had this image of myself on my journey in this life. I imagine that floating on top of the huge waves is a square platform of wood. I am standing on the platform, trying to balance, with no way to be safe. If I look in front of me, I see a snake. If I look behind, I see a lion. When I look on either side, I see fire. Where am I going to go? The water is very deep, and I cannot fly. I close my eyes, that blink and tear in the strong wind. I jump very quickly into the deep water. Sink or swim! There's no other way to survive. Try, cry, until you get there.

Now my story comes alive, flying higher toward the blue sky, painted in delicate colors by hand, just for me. I was reborn to love life, to see the smile of a child who caresses the flowers blooming on a spring day. Children play in the garden of love, touching pink roses with drops of dew like the tears of my Mamma, in the corner of her garden where the roses bloomed. The wind blew to me across the sea and kissed my face, whispering to me, "I love you, child." That love gave me hope that on rainy days I would once again breathe the scent of my mother's roses.

The butterfly flies to the sky where the stars shine above the moon, kissing every flower with the perfume of love. Their scent will last all through the winter months. My heart is as warm as the first day of spring, giving me the strength to go on. The same life that God gives to each bud that blooms with the beautiful face of each child, He gives back to me, to tell the story of my life.

Giovanna Maria Acciavatti

The Butterfly

The butterfly could not fly very high
without the luminous colors of her wings.

The wind picked up the baby from her crib
in the night of stormy weather.

The rain fell so fast in the darkness of the night.
The baby soared, far away from life,
to the blue sky.

Her white dress, painted by hand
with shining silk ribbons,
touched the harp while the angel played.

The baby danced with the angels in the open sky.
The baby found the luminous colors
to fly back to earth.

The baby butterfly, painted in the sky,
flew with her true colors,
of hope and joy of life
and love.

CHAPTER ONE

My Birth

*T*he little luminescent butterfly with the light of life in her heart continued her joyful flight down to earth. She was guided by a tiny angel with open wings, ready to sing a lullaby to the little butterfly, so helpless without her mamma—without her mamma's song, without her mamma's heart. The angel touched the butterfly, coloring her wings with the light of the sun, trying to shield her from the pain that was waiting for her.

Like a fragile-winged butterfly, I came out of my warm cocoon into the world. I unfolded my wings, but my wings were torn from the beginning. I couldn't fly. On a beautiful spring day, when the flowers were in bloom and the butterflies were flying from blossom to blossom to sip their nectar, I entered the world.

I was born the fourth child in a family of five children, to my Mamma, Lucia, and my Papà,

Fileno. I am privileged to share with you the story of my family: my beloved Mamma and Papà, my sisters, Adelina, Gabriella, and Maria, and my brother, Antonio. Papà worked for the railroad. Our house was right next to the train station in the ancient town of Loreto Aprutino, nestled in the hills among olive orchards and vineyards, in the Abruzzo region of Italy.

My parents welcomed my birth joyfully. My beautiful green eyes, like the emerald-green waters of the Adriatic Sea, were wide open, looking at my loving Mamma and Papà and all the children around me. Mamma took such good care of me, but when I reached the age of seven months, I was struck ill with a pneumonia as violent as the weather on the day I fell sick. Rain poured from the sky and the wind howled fiercely, blowing down the power lines outside. There was no electricity. As I lay gasping for the breath of life, the candles that cast light on my cold little body dripped wax onto the floor, like the tears of my family surrounding me and praying for my life.

In the dark of night, the torrential rain echoed the teardrops of my sorrowful Mamma, who was kneeling and wailing for her lifeless baby. The echo of her pain reached the little angel that hovered over my crib, trying to protect me from harm. Mamma

4

kept praying, kneeling in the flickering light.

When she became aware of the headlights of a train that was approaching fast in the distance, Mamma ran outside, lifting her arms to the sky. She desperately waved to stop the train, screaming for help, for a doctor. The train stopped at the station in front of our house. Miraculously, there was a doctor on board. He came into the house and examined me. Then he looked at Mamma hopelessly and said, *"La bimba è morta. Non posso fare niente!"* (The baby is dead. There is nothing I can do!) Mamma heard those words repeating in her head like a hammer. *"La bimba è morta, signora. La bimba è morta! Non c'è niente da fare. Non posso fare niente, mi perdoni!"*

Then there was silence. Mamma didn't hesitate. "Please, Doctor, don't let my daughter die! She can't die, she cannot be dead, please, I beg you!" Papà was banging his head against the wall in desperation. The neighbors were gathered, holding candles and kneeling around my lifeless little body, reciting the rosary. The powerful storm drenched the earth, as though the sky itself were crying. Confronted by such desperation, the doctor took a long needle out of his medical bag, and said, "I will try this injection and hope for a miracle." The doctor injected that painful shot into my lifeless body. The giant needle was my last chance for life.

The candles burning around my crib flamed higher. The praying and chanting of the people surrounding me filled the room and were joined by angels in the sky. The angels with their beautiful wings blew a miraculous wind of life, in the form of golden sparkles of light. After so many hours, my beautiful green eyes slowly reopened, and a small breath moved my little lungs. A tiny movement of my infant hands brought a loud response from the crowd. *"Miracolo! Miracolo!"* A real miracle happened. Tears of sadness and despair turned into tears of joy, especially for Mamma, whose heart started beating again!

What joy and relief for her, after she had lost her first-born child to the same illness, at a time when no cure was available. She suffered so much over his death that whenever it rained, she used to say, "I am going to the cemetery because my little boy is getting wet!" She would open an umbrella over the grave of her little son, as if he were alive and she needed to protect him from the storm and wind. She sold her clothes and jewelry to buy nearly life-size angel statues to place by his headstone. She believed that the angels would protect him from the cold nights. Those angel statues now stand guard at our family chapel in Loreto Aprutino.

After the stormy night when I rejoined my

family, Mamma went right away to the Church of San Gabriele, the Protector of Youths, in the mountains of Gran Sasso. At the church, she lit a votive candle for the mercy she had received. The little white coffin that my parents had ordered for me was donated to the church. My sister, Gabriella, wore a black uniform in thanks for the grace given to our family. For one long year, Gabriella wore this black dress, with a *stemma dorato* (coat of arms) on the breast, and long sleeves, even under the hot summer sun.

After the miracle that brought me back to life, I was a fragile and sickly child. When I fell down and hurt myself, I cried and cried to be picked up and comforted. But even with tears wetting my face, I always saw in front of my eyes that magical butterfly high in the sky. When I tried to touch it, I imagined that I was climbing up into the sky too, but then, all of a sudden, I fell back to earth and was hurt again. But my shining butterfly was still there for me, helping me fly higher in the face of pain and despair, and giving me the strength to go on.

As I grew up, I was treated like a delicate rose inside a crystal bell jar, where I tried to restore my torn wings so that I could chase the colors of the sky and touch the sun. But that safe crystal bell jar that protected me from harm and pain in my childhood would shatter into a million grains of sand. After all

the love and care my family gave me, I never expected to go through so much pain.

CHAPTER TWO

My Family

$\mathcal{M}$y mother, Lucia, was born in Civitella Casanova, a small town in the Abruzzo region of Italy. Her mother, Mariana, and her father, Alfonso, had three beautiful little girls. In the 1890s, they were living in a little house near the *piazza*, where they would sometimes stroll. They were very poor. After many years of struggling, my grandfather received a letter from some long-lost relatives who had emigrated to the United States. They told him that he could earn money there, and they sent him the necessary documents so that he could come to America, the land of opportunity. He had to say goodbye to his wife and his young daughters—my mamma and her sisters. As he waved goodbye, the tears rolled down his face, but he held onto a fierce dream of a better future for his family.

My grandfather Alfonso made the long journey by steamship to find work in America, in order to support his family. He first traveled to Naples, where an enormous ship was docked at the port, with crowds of people hovering near the steps, waiting to board. In steerage class, the passengers were crowded into berths in one large room. If the weather was good, they could spend time on the open deck. This deck, which had no covering, also served as a cafeteria. The wind would pick up the aluminum dishes from the tables and blow them around. Everyone had to run to catch the flying dishes and then clean them in the icy salt water. There was a communal bathroom to be shared by all, with almost no privacy. The conditions in steerage were miserable, and the passengers were covered with lice and dirt. Often, as they tried to talk to one another to pass the time, the ship heaved and rocked from the turbulent ocean, making it nearly impossible to speak. Day after day, men, women, and children lay in the berths or stood on the deck, gazing at the space between the sky and the water, looking to the faraway land.

When they arrived at the Port of New York, the passengers had to stand in line under the grey sky, waiting to be sprayed with disinfectant. Then they were put into quarantine on Ellis Island. Any passenger who was ill and didn't get better quickly would be sent all the way back home on the next ship. My grandfather was healthy, and was able to pass through the quarantine. The family that had sent him the necessary papers also provided him with a place to stay and some food. With their help, he landed a job working on the railroad near Philadelphia.

His letters to my grandmother would take a couple of months to arrive, and every once in a while there was one dollar in the mail. My grandmother waited and waited for that dollar to buy food for her three little daughters. One time, she waited and waited, in vain, to hear from him. Finally, she walked the long distance to the center of town to find out news about her husband, but no letter had arrived.

The next time the mail was expected, my grandmother sent a neighbor to ask for the letter from her husband. The neighbor went to get the mail and came back with an envelope, which bore a stamp from the United States. My grandmother was eager to see what was written in the letter, but the man ripped it up before she could read it. The letter was from the railroad company, informing my grandmother that my grandfather had died. Besides the letter, there was nothing in the envelope, not even one dollar for his family.

Everything was lost: a life, a husband and father, and a grandfather. Where could she turn for help? It was the end of the poor little family. My grandmother was desperate. She had no money and no food to give to her children. The family shivered from the cold and snow outside. My grandmother tried to feed her daughters the best she could, but it wasn't enough. My mamma and her sisters shared one little ceramic doll to play with. One day, they fought over the doll and wouldn't take turns playing with it. They pulled at it until they broke the doll, and then my poor grandmother cried along with them. Watching her children weep over the broken doll only increased her sadness and despair.

One day at school, my mamma said to the little girl who shared her desk, "Come home with me! Mamma will cook lunch for us!" When they got there, she announced, "Mamma, I've brought a friend to eat lunch with us." My grandmother picked up an empty dish and put it on the table, saying, "I have an extra dish, but no food to put on it." My mamma cried with disappointment, but she had to say goodbye to her little friend, who went back to her own house for lunch.

My grandmother realized she had to choose the best solution for everybody. That meant sending one of her children to the nuns. My grandmother looked at her three girls, and she felt torn into three pieces. Which child should she choose?

In the end, she decided to send her oldest daughter, and that is how my mother, Lucia, ended up in the faraway convent. She was still a small child when she entered the convent, and she stayed with the nuns until she was a grown-up young lady. When she left she was just a little girl, looking like an angel, with her long curly hair blowing in the summer breeze and the birds singing after her from their nests.

The convent was high up in the hills, far from the neighboring town. Every week, after the celebration of the mass, the nuns took all the girls into an open field of green grass to play. The little girls circled and ran around on the grass, laughing and singing prayers with the nuns, and chanting "ring around the roses." These spirited little children felt the grass under their feet only on Sundays.

Reciting the rosary, they followed the road back to the convent on the hill. When they arrived, they had a simple lunch. They set the long tables with aluminum dishes in the cold room, illuminated only by a little window high up on the wall. In silence, they prayed to say thanks for the meal. After lunch, the girls cleared their own plates, and went to have their lessons with the nuns. Later in the afternoon, everyone went to the chapel to pray and sing. Mamma loved music and loved to sing. She would sneak into the chapel before daylight to learn the music so she could sing along in church.

The nuns were very strict, and no complaining was allowed. When a girl had her time of the month, she'd have to pretend and say, "I have an upset stomach." The nuns would give her *olio di rigino* (castor oil), and then the poor girl really would feel sick, lying in her cold room.

But Mamma never criticized the nuns. She had a good sense of humor and she was very funny. With her lively personality, she quickly became involved with the theatre group in the convent. Mamma was a little bit *birichina* (mischievous), and loved to make people laugh. During prayers, the little girls knelt in front of their chairs, but Mamma sometimes crawled under the bed and pulled their legs. The other girls ran away, holding their chairs in front of them. Once, Mamma chased them to try to stop them, but she ran right into a wall and cut her head. The nuns stitched up her head with thick black thread, and punished her for her bad behavior. With stitches in her head, she had to scrub the floors and wash all the dishes for one long week.

While she was in the convent, Mamma couldn't see her own mother for years at a time, since the distance was very far and the carriage to take her home to visit rarely arrived. She remained in the convent until she was twenty years old. By then, she was an elegant and well-educated young woman. After all the years living at the convent, she came to the decision to become a nun herself. She felt comfortable with the nuns, and convent life was the only life she knew. But when my grandmother heard this, she rushed to the convent and said to her daughter, "Wait! Don't make a hasty decision. Before you do this, you need to see something of the outside world!" Mamma was reluctant to leave, but she didn't dare disobey her mother. She said her goodbyes to the nuns and to the girls she had spent so many years with, and followed her mother.

Mamma left her safe life in the convent, her sacred spiritual world, to experience life in the city. She was sent to visit family in Loreto Aprutino. Because of her strict upbringing by the nuns, she had a different air and an unusual elegance. When she walked down the street, everyone noticed her. At church she met and became friends with two sisters, and the three of them opened a design boutique together in the town. The three talented young women designed and sewed everything themselves, and their elegant shop window attracted passersby to stop and look at their beautiful creations. These two sisters, Emilia and Grazietta, introduced Mamma to their brother, Fileno, a sweet and funny man who was to become Mamma's husband and our Papà. During their courtship, Papà was very determined to conquer my mother, *"la bella ed angelica Lucia"* (the beautiful and angelic Lucia), as he called her.

While he was courting her, Papà would do anything to get a look at Mamma's pale face. The design boutique had a balcony, where the three young women would sometimes sit. Papà often stood under the balcony, stretching his neck into the air to try to catch a glimpse of Mamma's face. Sometimes Papà's efforts to steal a look at her ended in calamity, such as the time he slipped, lost his balance, and fell into a pig pen. He struggled to find his balance, but the hill he was standing on was steep and slippery. Into the pen he slid, ending up covered in mud just like one of the pigs! Mamma laughed with Papà's sisters, amused and curious about his strange behavior. Papà started laughing too, happy to get the attention of mischievous Mamma, who was charmed by his sweet and genial ways.

Papà never gave up trying to get Mamma's attention. He climbed up onto the branch of a fig tree and took a fig in his mouth. All of a sudden, the branch broke and he fell to the ground, still holding the fig between his teeth! Everyone laughed, including him. He always had a good sense of humor. Another time, he tried to mount a horse to show off how well he could ride. Instead, he ended up on the other side of the horse! Later, he would tell us these funny stories so we could live those moments together. I will never forget all the tales and all the laughter while we were growing up!

One day, Papà invited Mamma to his family's villa and farm in Loreto Aprutino, filled with olive trees, fruit trees, vineyards, and stables with horses and other animals. He wanted to show off to her the estate his father owned and had created for his family after his success in the United States.

My paternal grandfather, Antonio, was born in Loreto Aprutino, the only son in his family. In 1900, he was sent to Boston to visit some relatives and to start working in construction, building bridges. He was strong and brave in his dream of traveling to distant America, but to get there, he had to go through the same pain and struggles as my maternal grandfather, Alfonso. Papagrosso, as we called him, also made the long, miserable journey in steerage class on a huge steamship, and he too stayed in quarantine on Ellis Island, praying to God to let him stay in America, the land of opportunity.

In Boston, Antonio met some of his *compaesani*—men from his own region in Italy. He and his coworkers had to walk many hours to go to work in the morning. They decided to rent a garage closer to work. The garage had no heat or water, and there was only a *baccaus'* (outhouse) behind it. During the winter, the men slept in their clothes on the cold floor of the garage and woke up as frozen and stiff as snowmen. Even Antonio's mustache froze, all curled up like *calamari* (squid) in the frying pan!

Each time Papagrosso received his pay, he sent most of it to Nonna Giovina. She put aside some of the money to buy land when Papagrosso finally came back home to live. Papagrosso also sent packages with fancy lace underwear for Nonna Giovina, and chocolate, peanuts, and delicious marmalade for the children. When he arrived for a visit, it was a grand occasion. In the town *piazza*, a carriage with two horses was ready and waiting for this American *cavaliere* to get off the train. All the neighbors would run to look out the window and whisper excitedly, *"Un Americano è arrivato!"* Elbowing each other out of the way, they'd say, "Move over, let me see! *Ma chi è?* Who is it? It's Acciavatti! What a handsome man! *Ma, che bel'uomo!"*

Each time Papagrosso came home on the steamship to visit, he would make love to Nonna. That was the part they were waiting for! They had three children: my father, Fileno, and my aunts, Emilia and Grazietta. Their first-born, Adelina, had died of Spanish fever at the age of seventeen. Before she died, she asked my father to make a promise. "When I'm dead, come to my grave and say goodnight." For years, my father went to the chapel in Loreto Aprutino every night, to say, *"Adelina, buona notte! Vado a casa."* (Adelina, good night! I'm going home). But one night at the cemetery, he saw a pure white dog appear out of the mist, sitting on Adelina's grave. Terrified, he fled for home and told Mamma what he had seen. He never went back. But our family always remembered to put flowers on Adelina's grave when we visited the cemetery.

When my grandfather finally went back to Italy for good, he bought the villa in Loreto Aprutino and moved his family there. The abundance of the farm was like a cornucopia, with huge overflowing baskets of fruits and vegetables for every taste. My grandparents were generous and gave food to anyone who needed it. Every week, Nonna filled baskets with fresh produce, cheese, and bread, and went to the piazza, where she gave out food to people who were less fortunate. The villa was filled with the pleasures of cooking for family, friends, and neighbors—full of love and laughter!

After a long courtship, Papà found the courage to propose. He went to the nuns at the convent to ask for Mamma's hand in marriage. Together, Papà and Mamma spoke privately with the Mother

Superior. The nuns approved and gave the couple their blessing. They watched the young couple until they disappeared into the colorful world, and then they turned and went back to their sequestered life in the convent.

The marriage took place at the villa in Loreto Aprutino, with all the family present, including the nuns. Mamma appeared in a long white wedding dress that she had designed herself. On her hair was a crown of white *fiori d'aranci* (orange blossoms). Beautiful white flowers were spread on the *terrazza* to celebrate this pure moment of love—the union of two hearts, two families, two different worlds— but under the same sky. The bells rang with joyous sounds. The train of Mamma's gown was so long that it stretched along the path all the way to the stone steps, which were covered with overflowing baskets of pure-white orange blossoms. All the guests stood and applauded her majestic pose. After the ceremony, there was a huge feast, followed by delicious homemade pastries and the traditional wedding *confetti* (sugared almonds) in baskets filled to the brim and tied with ribbons the color of the sky. The champagne was opened to the sound of music. As they danced slowly under the open sky, the guests raised their glasses to wish good luck to the beautiful couple. After the party, the newlyweds rode to the train station in a carriage decorated with silk ribbons tied to the bridles of the white horses that pulled it. The carriage was draped with a lace cover, adorned with pearl droplets dangling from the lace.

The honeymoon was in romantic Venice, on the canals with their unforgettable gondolas. At that time it was a great privilege to travel to such a fancy, expensive, and elegant city. Because of Papa's job with the railroad, the couple were able to travel comfortably in the first-class car, where they had plenty of space to enjoy the long trip among the rich red velvet upholstery.

It was the dream of every couple, and my parents, with joy in their hearts, heard the notes of the music of love. Venice, the city of the gondolas of lovers! Venice, the city of *merletti* (lace), Murano glass, the Carnival masks! The young couple spent one glorious week in the city known as *La Serenissima* (The Most Serene). Then they traveled to nearby Treviso, to stay with Papà's cousins for one more week. When the newlyweds arrived, the cousins, wearing traditional Venetian costumes, were waiting to give them a beautiful feast. The table was set with a lace tablecloth and baskets of fresh flowers cut from their garden. The guests drank champagne from elegant, long-stemmed glasses and sang and danced late into the night.

After a lovely honeymoon, Mamma and Papà settled into a big house in Loreto Aprutino, right next to the railroad station. A long *viale* (avenue) of tall, fragrant pine trees led to the house from the road. Papà worked for the electric railroad, the Linea Pescara-Penne, which traveled between the towns of Pescara and Penne, near the Adriatic coast. Mamma began to use all her talents to make a beautiful, comfortable home for her family.

CHAPTER THREE

My Childhood

Out of my parents' passionate love for each other, Mamma gave birth to five children: four girls and one boy, the "king" of the family. She was a delicate woman, so during each pregnancy she was confined to bed. Papà had to hire a woman to scrub the laundry by hand and clean the house. Before he went to work, he called on some of Mamma's friends—Signora Mimi, Signora Cartiera, who had a printing business, and Signora Maria—to come keep Mamma company and bring her cups of tea as she sat propped up in bed.

Mamma and Papà loved us more than themselves. We were a family with God in our hearts, because Mamma had spent so many years in the convent. It was an advantage for us that Mamma had been well educated by the nuns. In everyday life, our family was thankful and lived by the word of God.

Papà was a tall, happy, handsome man with a

23

full head of curly chestnut-brown hair. His eyes, like Mamma's, were the aquamarine color of the waters of the Adriatic Sea. I remember him most of all as a family man, a gentleman who treated Mamma like a queen. He was a devoted husband and father to his wife and five children.

During her life in the convent, Mamma had always loved to sing, and she wanted to teach her own children to sing together as a family. With a pure soprano voice, she taught us to sing songs together, just like the Trapp Family in *The Sound of Music*. She sewed and embroidered clothes for us by hand, and dressed us like little dolls, making sure we looked beautiful, with flowers in our hair. When it was time to sing, my brother Antonio stood in the middle, in his hand-embroidered suit, and we girls gathered around him. Mamma, holding a piece of lace in her hands, conducted us as we sang:

Qui tra nastri e merletti
Le stoffe e le trine
Qui le vispe sartorine
Stanno insieme a lavorare.
Lavoriamo domani sera,
Lavoriamo la notte ancora!
Ma la gioia più sincera
Rallegra i nostri cuori!

(Here among the ribbons and lace,
The fabric and the filet,
Here the sprightly seamstresses
Gather together to work.
Let us work tomorrow evening,
Let us work in the night also!
But joy most sincere
Brightens our hearts!)

Mamma's angelic voice lured the nuns from the convent over to our house to visit. They arrived pumping a railroad handcart, their black gowns billowing like umbrellas. They held onto their nuns' caps with one hand, so as not to show their bald heads, which they had shaved as young novices. The nuns sat with us in our rose garden, sipping rose-flavored tea from porcelain cups and remembering old times. Mamma also frequently invited some of her classmates from the convent to join the tea party. The adults asked us to sit with them in the garden while they told stories and laughed about their years with the nuns. My mischievous brother, Antonio, hid behind the door, making fun of how they sipped their tea! Mamma usually served some cold *bevande gazzose* (sparkling beverages) to refresh their tongues from all that talking.

When the grownups went indoors for a little

while, we children would sometimes hide under the table and wait for the nuns to sit down again. We wanted to find out if the nuns were wearing underwear! This was a question that I was curious about during my entire childhood. As I grew older, I loved to sit with the adults in the corner of the garden, where the warm sun brought forth the intoxicating perfume of the roses.

With her royal pose, my little Mamma looked like a queen, dressed in handmade white lace dresses that she sewed herself. She often wore an embroidered collar and cultured pearls around her long white neck, enhancing her natural beauty. In the summer, she gathered her hair on one side with a filigreed tortoise-shell comb, so that her silky, curly hair framed her pale face like an angel's. Her heart-shaped red lips stood out like precious rubies. Her eyes, as green as the waves of the Adriatic Sea, communicated her kind soul. Mamma's sweet and caring eyes looked at me, *la piccola Giovanna*, while she sang lullabies and caressed me with her soft, delicate hands.

Mamma was a very religious woman and recited the rosary every night in solitude. She was a great homemaker and mother, and a skilled clothing designer as well. After she married, she dedicated hours to designing clothes and teaching religious doctrine to children. As a child, I remember so well Mamma looking at me, saying teasingly, "Giovanna, my little nun, you would look very cute with your round face in the nun's veil." I would cry, "No, no! I don't want to be a nun!" And I'd run away!

Our house had three bedrooms, two living rooms, two bathrooms (one inside and one outside), and a huge kitchen with marble countertops, where my family spent most of our time together. I remember standing on a stool, surrounded by my brother and sisters, all of us watching our parents cooking delicious food for our dinner. We children tried to imitate our parents and pretended to cook too. We would try to make pasta, but made a mess of flour instead! When the white flour spilled onto the red ceramic floor tiles, it looked so pretty, just like a decoration. Papa would take a little lock of my hair in his fingers and ask teasingly, *"Ma che fai? Ch'è successo?"* (What are you doing? What happened?)

The furniture in Mamma and Papà's bedroom was from our grandparents' villa in Loreto Aprutino. In the corner stood a big armoire with mirrored doors and drawers below. One day, my little sister, Maria, and I decided that we wanted to see who was taller. We opened one of the drawers of the armoire and climbed onto it to look at ourselves in the mirror. But the armoire fell forward onto us, pinning us underneath it. We yelled and screamed for help! We had to wait for someone to rescue us, and—at least that day—we didn't find out who was taller.

My grandparents both died young, so I didn't have the chance to know them for long, but our visits to the villa with its rooms filled with beautiful paintings and elegant furnishings always restored me with their harmony. At the villa, I loved to sleep in the embroidered sheets, among my grandmother's lace underthings. In the morning, I heard the sonorous chimes of the grandfather clock, standing tall downstairs among the antique furniture. I felt peaceful as I lay in the big bed, looking through the delicate curtains that covered the windows and watching the small movements of the birds in the trees through the lace.

At home, when Mamma woke us in the morning, she always said, *"Chi è Giovanna? Gabriella? Adelina, Maria e Antonio? Cari miei bimbi, voi siete tutti un viso unico bello!"* (Who is Giovanna? Gabriella? Adelina, Maria and Antonio? My dear little children, each of you has a unique and beautiful face!) Whenever we had to get up to go to school to study with the nuns, Mamma sang a special little song. She thought I was asleep, but I was already awake because I wanted to hear her singing:

"Non sarà più la tua mammina
che ti sveglia la mattina,
ma sarà la monachina
col bacio di Gesù."

(No longer will it be your little mamma
who wakes you in the morning,
but it will be the little nun,
with a kiss from Jesus.)

Later, my sister Maria was sent to a convent school in Rome for several years. Whenever Maria was visiting home and it was time to go back to the convent, Mamma always sang this little song to her. The convent school was very fancy, and the nuns fed the girls on rich cheese, bread, and meat every day, so that the girls would get too fat to be attractive, and would become nuns too. One day, when Mamma went to visit Maria at the convent, she saw that her youngest daughter was starting to become very plump, and that was the end of Maria's stay with the nuns!

Very early each morning, Papà started the fire in the kitchen fireplace. As we came down the stairs, he whispered, *"Fatte piano, che la mamma dorme."* (Be quiet, so your mother can sleep.) *"Buon giorno, Papà,"* we greeted him, and he waited for a well-deserved kiss from each of us. He kissed us on our foreheads and then picked up each of us and carried us over to the fireplace, where fragrant pine cones were burning in the fire. We sat and warmed ourselves while Papà prepared breakfast for all of us, humming opera tunes under his breath. Caffè latte made with fresh milk, toasted bread, and *biscotti di pasta frolla* (shortbread cookies) were ready on the table. When the milk can was opened, there was a pop! The milk was still warm and bubbling from the cows on our farm. After we had breakfast together, Papà went off to work at the electric railroad. He warned us, *"Non fate arrabbiare Mamma! Mi raccomando!"* (Don't make Mamma angry! I'm warning you!) And we said, "Don't worry, Papà, be calm at work and don't worry about Mamma."

I remember waiting for Papà's phone call, staring at the big mahogany telephone hanging on the wall. It used morse code and had two receivers: one was long and one was small and round. Our phone number was one long ring—two short rings—one long ring. Almost no one had that type of phone in Italy at the time. We were lucky to have one because Papà worked for the railroad. I would run to answer the phone, climb up on a stool and pick up the small receiver in my little hands. Feeling like such a big girl, I said into it, *"Pronto, Papà!"* (Hello, Papa!). I was so happy to hear his voice! He'd say, "How do you feel, baby?" And I answered, "Papà, where are you? I'm waiting for you! Come home!"

Papà always called to me, *"Giovanna, figlia di Papà, vieni qui, dolcezza!"* (Giovanna, Papà's daughter, come here, my sweetness!) My brother and sisters were jealous of me—little Giovanna, getting so much attention. But my brother always protected me like a little gentleman, in his own unique and gentle way.

We also had a gramophone, with a mahogany base. The wood of the turntable, where the records lay, was a little darker than the rest. The speaker was a gigantic brass bell in the shape of a lily, covered in filigree. The records were big and heavy! You had to turn a crank to play the music, so that people could dance. But very often, the needle skipped and played the same notes over and over. I watched curiously from the upstairs landing as the dancers tried to waltz to the music with one foot raised, waiting for the song to continue. I felt such excitement, peeking through the banisters to see what was happening downstairs. To me, the music was like a romantic lullaby. When I finally got into bed, I went to sleep and dreamed about a handsome prince on a white horse.

I used to go to sleep with my hands crossed over my chest, waiting for the chubby little angel who protected me to come and sleep with me in my bed. Sometimes, while I was trying to make room for the angel to lie down, I would roll out of bed and fall on the floor! Then I cried to be carried to my parents' bed.

Because of my fragile health, I was treated like a delicate rose under a crystal bell jar. But every day, that delicate flower had to face the torture of the long needle piercing my body. There were moments when I couldn't breathe from asthma attacks and had to raise my arms to catch a breath of air. I became anxious and cried. When the doctor came each day to give me that painful injection, I fought him with all the strength in my little body.

Being forced by the doctor to have those daily shots was traumatic for me. I felt that my body was abused every day, when the doctor made me take down my underwear. The doctor pulled down my underwear, and I pulled it up—up and down, up and down. I thought he wanted to look at my *culetto* (behind). The doctor would exclaim to Mamma in frustration, *"Ma questa bimba, Signora!"* Sometimes a neighbor, Giseppa, who was a nurse, came to give me the shot. Mamma told me later that I screamed and cried when I recognized Giseppa's footsteps on the staircase. Mamma was concerned and she called Papà to calm me down. I sat at the window of my parents' bedroom, anxiously waiting to see my father's figure coming home through the pine trees to help comfort my childhood fear. Papà came home to hold me in his arms during that painful injection. For me, that was love, and that was all I needed.

My siblings teasingly called me *scolapasta* (colander) because of all the holes in my body from the injections. Because of my ill health, I had to have those shots from infancy until I was nine years old. I was frequently sick with asthma and bronchitis and I often cried from pain. This painful life prevented me from enjoying a normal childhood. Mamma often told my brother and sisters not to bother me. "Be careful! She's not well! *È l'avanzo della morte!* (She's the leftover death!) Don't make her cry!"

When my illnesses flared up, I had difficulty breathing and Mamma had to sit next to my bed to watch over me. I didn't want to eat. Mamma told me to open my mouth for the spoon, or else the angels would cry! I remember sitting in a high chair while my parents were frying potatoes for the family. Mamma put a little piece of delicious fried potato on my chair. Then a miracle happened. My fingers began moving towards the potato and I started to put it in my mouth. Mamma said quietly to Papà, "Shh! Don't look at her! Just put another little piece of potato on the chair!" After few seconds, my mouth was munching.

Ever since then, Mama often told me the story of the potato. "Giovannella, we found you under the potato plant!" Sometimes, when we were riding in the bus, Mamma would say to me, "Listen! There is a little baby girl who is crying. I can't see her. Where is she? Look carefully, under that potato plant. There she is! We'll bring her home and take care of her." To this day, when I feel depressed or sad, I eat my favorite food: *la patata*. The potato is my comfort food.

My brother and sisters and I spent long days outside under the emerald-green, perfumed pine trees, where our Papà had built swings hung with tall ropes from their branches. Their pinecones dropped from the trees onto the long avenue to our house. They opened as soon as they landed, and we played with them on the grass. We opened the cones and ate the white *pignoli* nuts, savoring their delicate flavor.

When Antonio was five or six years old, he climbed up and down one of the pine trees like a little squirrel, carrying a small piece of wood each time. After a while, he had made a miniature house in the tree. He told Papà, "I built a villa for my wife! That's where I'm going to bring her to make love to her!"

Outside our kitchen window was a huge

grapevine. One day, Papà brought a chair outside and climbed up on it to pick some grapes that were too high for him to reach. The chair slipped out from under him and he fell onto the ground! We kids started laughing at him. He couldn't help laughing too, saying in mock outrage, "Hey, isn't anyone going to help me?"

I learned at a young age to take advantage of my weakness to get what I wanted. I wanted my family to hug me and and love me and take care of me in every sense of the word. When the time came to take turns playing on the swing in our back yard, I wouldn't stop swinging to let my siblings have a turn. I left my sisters waiting, saying, "Sorry, the swing won't stop! I can't do anything about it. I have to continue. If you stop me, I will tell Papà!" My brother Antonio called me *la spia* (the telltale). "If we catch you, you are done!" they would say. But when they caught me, they kissed me!

I loved the special attention when my sisters kissed my little feet, tickling me. If I woke up first in the morning, I crept as slowly and quietly as I could, and pulled my sisters' toes while they were still asleep, tickling them while I pulled the pillows from under them. Then we'd start to play, throwing and pulling the pillows until they opened up and the feathers flew all over the place! They stuck to our hair and our lips as we tried to kiss each other, like the little birds that fly together in their happy families.

Whenever there was a festival in our town, Mamma and Papà took us to watch the celebration. At the *gelateria* (ice cream shop) in the piazza, Papa would buy each of us a *gelato,* a Bacio Perugina, and a balloon. Papà often carried me on his back because I tired easily. One time, after I'd eaten my ice cream and candy, I pestered Papà for another Bacio, but I got a little spanking instead. Then my balloon broke and I howled! Papà told Maria to give me her balloon, even though she was the youngest.

Because I was a "miracle baby," one Easter, Mamma decided that I should walk in the procession for *Venerdi Santo* (Good Friday) in Loreto Aprutino. She and Adelina spent weeks embroidering my clothes for the occasion: not only my dress, but also my underwear, socks, and hat.

Gabriella always carried the cross for me. Mamma told her to go the auction in the Church of San Rocco. At only six years old, she was sent to bid on a little whip for me to carry in the Good Friday procession. She had spunk and spirit, and as young she was, she bravely shouted out *"Cento lire!"* (one hundred lire!)

I remember being dressed up in the fancy embroidered outfit, all decked out like a wax doll. As

I walked in the procession, I heard my Mamma and Papà and sisters calling out to me, "Giovaaan-naaaaa!" They were so happy and proud for me, blowing kisses and clapping their hands. I heard them yelling and felt a sudden rush of embarrassment course through my body. I sat down abruptly on the sidewalk and took off my fancy shoes and socks. I refused to walk any further, and cried and cried to be picked up. In the end, Gabriella took my place, and I was held and comforted in the safety of my father's arms.

Papà was one of the famous Bersaglieri, the light infantry of the Italian Army, who wore blue uniforms and dashing broad-brimmed hats decorated with long plumes of black capercaillie feathers flowing down the right side. It was thrilling to see them as they paraded through the streets of Loreto Aprutino, playing their trumpets and stepping perfectly in time. They marched down the avenue as the people cheered and threw rose petals. I remember hearing the women in the crowd talking excitedly about the beautiful young men in their uniforms! *Che bello!*

When we were old enough, we helped Mamma by working in the *biglietteria* (ticket booth) that was right next to our house, selling train tickets to passengers. Sometimes there were crowds of people, and it was hard to keep track of the money. When Papà came to the biglietteria at the end of the day, he would check the money. Sometimes he asked, "Who sold the tickets today? Giovanna? Maria? Who? There are twenty *soldi* missing!"

Across the street from the station was a little delicatessen that also belonged to our family. There we sold everything from A to Z: wine, beer, soda, *panini* (sandwiches), cigarettes, and assorted household items. After Papà applied for a business license, we built the store ourselves on a small plot of land that Papà was able to buy at a good price. When we started to build the store, I was the only child who was at home to help. My sisters were away at school, and Antonio was already married, with a young son. I quit school temporarily to help with the store. To get the business going right away, we started to run it out of our own kitchen. Mamma was always busy in the kitchen, already selling goods, running from one place to another. She wore her hair in a braid wrapped around her head, and her dresses always had a v-neck, finished with embroidery.

I was a young teenager, enjoying all the activity. I rode my bicycle back and forth with buckets of water so the workers could mix the cement to build the store. It was fun to fly down the street on my bike carrying the water bucket, my ponytail flying in the wind. The water from the bucket splashed onto my legs and cooled me off. Behind our house, Papà had set up and decorated a little place for me to cook. At about 3:00 p.m., I had to start cooking for the men who would come after work to eat before they got on the train to go home. When the store was finally ready, we held a grand opening party. My parents hired an orchestra from Loreto Aprutino, and all the guests danced under the open sky to celebrate our new business.

Once the store was up and running, I went back to school, and things returned to normal. Later, Gabriella was married in a beautiful wedding ceremony in our *viale dei pini*, under the pine trees. Maria had come back from the convent, happy to be home.

We were all very busy selling tickets in the biglietteria, cooking, cleaning, and working in the store, too. Sometimes we had to pick up a message from the train conductor concerning a change of schedule. We stood at the door, waiting for the train to stop at our station. When the conductor gave us the information, we had to leave a note on the station door with the new schedule. We were so young, and of course, we needed to break some rules occasionally! Once, when we were supposed to be waiting for the train, we girls stole a cigarette from our store and hid in the bedroom, secretly taking puffs. One puff for you, one for me! We were having fun, chatting and laughing, lying on the bed together. Our bed was silver and brass, with brass bedknobs. It had a big flower design pressed into the headboard, which was very difficult to polish. When it was time to clean our bedroom, we flipped a coin to see who would have to polish the bed!

Smoking in our bedroom was a very daring thing to do. Mamma smelled the smoke and followed the yellow brick road. She ran upstairs, calling, "Girls! What's that smell? What are you doing? Open the door!" She pulled at the doorknob and it came off in her hands! We had to open the door from the inside. Mamma was beside herself. She charged into the darkened room, waving her hands in the smoke. She couldn't see anything. "Wait till Papà comes home!" she cried. Just then the train arrived and no one was outside to meet it! From the bedroom window, we just waved and called, "*Ciao! See you later!*" Mamma was furious, but we couldn't stop laughing!

There were always young men hanging around in the street, between the train station and our delicatessen. When we girls were working in the store, sometimes Papà would send us back to the train station to get us away from the young men. But as soon as we went back to the biglietteria, the young men followed us home anyway! *Che pena, Papà!* Our poor father didn't know what to do with us!

CHAPTER FOUR

Family Traditions

*I*n my family, Mamma was the fulcrum and Papà was the rock. Every Sunday, the family had midday dinner together. My parents, who loved to cook together, prepared many different dishes. One of our favorites was *pasta alla chitarra* (egg pasta), a specialty of the Abruzzo region, accompanied by sophisticated side dishes. *La salsa mista*, for example, was a side dish made of different types of meats (veal, pork, and beef) prepared in the shape of *involtini* (rolls), often with sausage as a filling.

On Sundays, while our parents were cooking, my sisters and I went to church to hear the *Santa Messa* (Sacred Mass). We decked ourselves out in our fancy clothes, handmade from silk chiffon and lace. As we fastened onto our heads delicate lace veils, *trapuntato à rilievo e smerlato* (quilted in relief and scalloped), we heard the bells ringing for the mass. We joined our neighbors and friends in church, ready for the daily prayer. As we listened to music from the organ and the choir, especially the pure voices of the little boys, I felt my heart touched with joy and pain. The nuns sang too, with their angelic voices. After confession, when the time came to receive the sacred host at Communion, we were careful not to chew it, but kept it safely on our palates until it dissolved.

When my parents had almost finished cooking, Mamma looked out the window to see if we were returning and said to Papà, "Fileno, dear, put the pasta in the pot. The girls are coming back!" Papà was the master chef! He was a fanatic in the kitchen, and when he made coffee, the *miscela di caffè* (coffee blend) was mixed from three different kinds of espresso. In the afternoon, Papà would make *caffè corretto* with a dash of anisette liqueur. I can still smell the caffè and see Papà sipping from his cup.

The Sunday tradition was an intimate way to express our love for each other and to strengthen our family unity. Each Sunday there was a different menu. When we were older, each family member took a turn cooking the meal. A favorite dish was *minestrone*, a soup made with fresh vegetables picked from our garden. Another delicious soup was *stracciatella con vitello e agnello* (egg drop soup with veal and lamb) *gnocchi di patate* (potato dumplings) and *crochette* shaped like little flowers. For a main dish, we might have *arrosti di carne mista con cardoni* (roasted meats mixed with celery) served with fresh eggs. *La cicoria* (chicory) was simmered along with slices of thick *pancetta* from the pork raised on our family's farm in Loreto Aprutino. Other popular dishes were *manicotti ripieni con spinacci* (manicotti stuffed with spinach) and *mozzarella tartufo* (mozzarella cheese with truffles).

Nidi di rondine (swallow's nests) was a special treat. We rolled pasta dough into a big sheet on the table, and spread it with *salsa Genovese*—tomato sauce with carrots and a little chopped meat. Then we rolled the dough into one long roll, and cut it into three-inch slices. We covered the slices with *besciamella* (béchamel sauce), mozzarella, and parmigiano, and baked it in the oven. *Delizioso!*

Over the fire, we cooked *pizza al forno,* made from yellow cornmeal with layers of mozzarella, topped with olive oil and rosemary. We made little impressions in the dough with our fingers, so that the fragrant oil pooled inside them. We ate the pizza with *contorno prosciutto* (vegetables with thinly sliced, dry-cured ham). For our main course we had *vitello arrostito* (roasted veal) or *pollo ripiena con pancetta e pane arrostito* (chicken stuffed with thin slices of ham), and *funghi trifolati* (fresh mushrooms), picked under the trees on the farm and sautéed with garlic and onions. Their delicate, earthy flavor was unforgettable.

When Papà was transferred to a different railroad station, our family moved to the town of Capelle, where we lived in another big house next to the station, also with a long avenue of fragrant pine trees leading to the house. Every day, the *contadini* (farmers) brought fresh vegetables, fruits, eggs, cheeses and much more from the *campagna* (countryside) as gifts for Mamma. The farmers looked like the Three Kings paying tribute to the baby Jesus! They always came to our Mamma first, to give her the best produce, meats, and cheeses. In addition, all the produce and livestock from our family farm in Loreto Aprutino was divided into three parts, to be shared between Papà and his two sisters. Every year, we received huge containers of olive oil from the olive trees at the villa.

Mamma was honored and respected as the matriarch, not only of our family, but of the whole town. Not only was she a wonderful homemaker and mother, but she was also an excellent teacher, finding time to teach embroidery to young girls from the surrounding area. Her designs and embroidery decorated the stoles that the priests wore at our church, as well as the beautiful silk coverings for the altar.

Mamma taught catechism too, and did her best to recreate all the experiences she'd had with the nuns. Mamma would tell the neighborhood children all about growing up in the convent, enchanting them with her stories. Papà, especially, never tired of listening to Mamma recounting tales about her years in the convent.

On the weekends, we rode our bicycles under the watchful eyes of our parents, or we went to the movies in Loreto Aprutino, accompanied by our mother. After the movies, Mamma always brought us to the Pasticceria Rienzi for delicious pastries. Our favorite was *bombe alla crema* (cream-filled doughnuts). When we arrived, the owner of the Pasticceria always said, "Here comes Lucia with her little chicks!" Mamma would call Papà on the phone and tell him, "We'll be home at ten o'clock." He'd say, "All right! Dinner will be ready!" On the way to the station to take the train home to Capelle, we'd buy *calde roste* (roasted chestnuts) from a little cart. The vendor called, *"Buona sera! Sono caldi e sono buoni!"* (Good evening! They're hot and delicious!) He gave the chestnuts to us in a little paper cone. They were aromatic and warmed our hands and our stomachs. When we arrived home, the table was set and the house smelled wonderful. While we ate our dinner, Mamma would tell Papà all about the movie, describing the story and all the characters in detail.

Mamma used to tell us how, before any of us were born, she and Papà rode in a carriage to the movie theater, to see silent movies. Mamma put on a fancy hat with embroidered flowers, and Papà dressed up too. He wore a jacket over his vest, with a gold watch fob that went from his jacket to the watch in his vest pocket. When he wanted to check the time, he pulled out the watch and pushed a button to open the case.

Mamma said that it was hard to follow the story of the silent movies, because people were shifting in their seats and she couldn't always read the titles on the screen. Still, she sometimes told us the story of one of the films, and I would fall asleep and dream about it.

Many of my favorite memories are of the major holidays, although as I look back, every day with my family felt like a holiday. For these special occasions, all the foods were prepared by hand. For me, the most memorable holiday was *Pasqua* (Easter Sunday).

Two weeks before Easter, we started to bake. We used lots of fresh eggs and cheeses to make the sweets. The girls' sweets were in the shape of dolls, and there were horse-shaped sweets for the boys. The dough for the sweets was *pasta frolla* (shortbread), and they were decorated with many-colored candy *confetti*. The bodies of the horse-shaped sweets were made of a hard boiled egg surrounded by braids of pasta frolla. There were large cheesecakes, smelling of springtime and warm weather, as well as many other pastries, such as cheese puffs, *sfogliatelle* (shell-shaped pastries filled with sweetened ricotta), *tortine di pesche* (little cakes in the shape of peaches), and *crostate d'uva* (grape tarts).

When the church bells rang on the evening before Easter, my family carefully filled large *ceste* (baskets) with all the foods we had prepared with so much attention, and carried them to church for the Easter benediction by the priest.

The next morning, on Pasqua, the long table in my family's kitchen was all decked out with a long white lace tablecloth, crystal glasses, and sparkling silverware. At breakfast, we tasted all the food the priest had blessed the evening before. Holding one another's hands, we recited the Credo and then feasted on the delicious dishes, which tasted especially wonderful because they had been blessed.

At one o'clock, we had *pranzo* (lunch), which consisted of different types of warm broths with *tortellini* (filled pasta) or *cardoni* (cardoon, a vegetable related to celery). The main course was traditional roasted lamb with roasted potatoes. Another dish was made of eggs poured into square molds and baked in the oven. These square-shaped eggs were often added to the warm broths as well. An assortment of meats, called *arrosti*, were roasted in the fireplace. A great variety of fresh vegetables were served as side dishes and they decorated the abundant table, spread with *vivande squisite* (exquisite dishes).

We always obeyed our father's orders and tried to emulate his values of respecting others. At the table, Papà sat first and we followed. An important tradition at Pasqua was writing our letters to Papà. Each child wrote a grateful note to Papà and put it under his dish at the table. His was the only dish to be placed upside down, hiding our letters as a special gift to our devoted father. Papà, pretending to be surprised, always said, "Why is my dish upside down? What happened, Lucia?" Papà picked up and opened each letter, one at a time. Each child had to stand up and read his or her letter aloud. I always felt embarrassed when Papà asked me to read my letter. The reading of the letters in front of all the family was very emotional. Even now, the memory is so sweet that it brings me to tears.

At Pasqua, Papà would give each of us a *soldino* (penny), as well as *torroni e cioccolatini* (nougat and chocolate candies). We put them aside, next to our plates, and tried not to eat them! My brother and sisters always ended up eating their candies right away, but I saved mine to give to them later, at the end of the meal. I was happy to make them happy. I was a shy little girl, but also playful and full of life. I remember holding my father's nose in my fingers and moving it back and forth as if I were ringing a bell. That made everyone laugh!

The next day, *La Pasquetta*, we had a picnic on the fresh green spring grass with all the family, enjoying *lasagne al forno con pasta fatta in casa* (baked lasagne with homemade pasta), *timballo al forno* (baked timbale), *carni arrostite con patate* (roasted meats with potatoes), *focaccia* and *salsicce fatte in casa* (homemade sausages). Fresh *bevande* (beverages) and pastries were prepared all week long, to celebrate this holiday. Our family sang Italian songs together and invited friends to join us. When Pasqua was finally over, our lives went back to our normal routine.

March, the month of violets, brought the celebration of San Giuseppe. Then Mamma gave me and my sisters permission to go with our girlfriends into the woods. She dressed us in beautiful, bell-shaped "campanula" gowns, hand-made from Italian cotton in different colors: emerald green, sky blue and ivory. Those dresses were made with the talent and artistry of design that ran deep in our family's heritage.

On our left arms we carried big baskets with

long handles, as we wandered through the woods, picking the fresh, perfumed violets, whose colors were illuminated by golden rays of sunlight that filtered through the trees. We gathered as many violets as we could find, eager to bring their springtime perfume to our devoted Mamma, who was waiting anxiously for us at the front door of our house. She was always delightfully surprised and happy to receive our gifts of fragrant violets. The joy that emanated from her suffused our minds and hearts with the harmony of spring's blossoming colors.

March also brought the return of the *rondini* (swallows), which had left their nests in our garden the previous autumn, to migrate to Africa. They reappeared every year at the same time, on March 21st. Every time we opened the windows of our bedroom, we heard their joyful chirping, reminding us that spring was here. The soft sounds of their music in our ears rocked us like a lullaby. Their chirping almost seemed to speak to us, saying, "We are back! Spring is here!" What joy and happiness that was for us! The little swallows arrived, lighting on the tops of the pine trees, flying free with their tiny wings and kissing us with their beaks at the windows. They seemed so full of life, ready to return to their nests to fill their babies' beaks with food.

I loved to look up at my favorite flowering *mandorli* (almond trees), where the birds would flock and fly around, dancing at each blossom to show off their beautiful feathers. The mandorli blossoms were special flowers of my childhood. Their scent still lingered in my nostrils and all around me, every time I came back to America.

May, when the flowers blossomed, was the month of *Santa Maria, La Madonna* (Saint Mary the Virgin). During May, the family went to church together every weekend to pray. Mamma would also turn our living room into a sacred place for praying, often inviting the neighbors to join us. We children sat very close, in the first row, so that we could watch Mamma praying and singing. The singing always lulled me to sleep, so Papà would pick me up and carry me up to bed. One time, as he was carrying me in the dark, he forgot to feel for the bed before laying me down. He dropped me on the floor and, according to him, I sang an opera aria!

In May, it was our family's tradition to plant flowers in our garden. Each member of the family had a favorite flower. Mamma's was the tea rose. Antonio's flower was the orchid, Maria's was the violet, Gabriella's was the lilac, and Adelina's was the magnolia. Like Mamma's, mine was the rose—those dear roses that in the future I would receive tucked into Mamma's letters to me. The roses always blossomed in a special corner of the garden, for Mamma and me.

During the springtime, we girls sat in the garden to do embroidery on the *telaio* (loom), while our brother went to work with Papà. At dinner time, everyone gathered together to cook a delicious meal from scratch. Such wonderful *spezzatini* (stews), *minestroni* (soups), *gnocchi* (potato dumplings), and *polenta fatte in casa* (homemade polenta)! Mamma and Papà taught us how to cut the fresh pasta with a knife to make *tagliatelle* (flat noodles), and we became expert little chefs!

During the following summer months, life at our house was always lively. We were busy at the biglietteria, selling tickets for the trains on the Linea Pescara-Penne, that passed through our station. Every Sunday, Papà took the train all the way to Loreto Aprutino to buy *la migliore porchetta* (the best pork). This boneless pork dish is a specialty of Abruzzo and its taste was sublime! The tradition was to cut the pork into slices edged with crispy skin. As you bit into it, you felt as if you were in heaven. The pork slices were served with stuffed olives and all kinds of cheeses from the farm.

Summertime was also the season for vacationing. Our family usually took a few trips together, sometimes to Venice, Rome, or Naples. Occasionally, we went to Assisi to visit the Basilica of San Francesco D'Assisi, or to the Church of San Gabriele in the beautiful mountains of Gran Sasso. My father's company paid all the expenses for our trips, and we traveled in the first-class car, beautifully upholstered in rich red velvet.

At Ferragosto, on August 31st, the *Circuito di Pescara*—the famous auto race—took place. All the streets were closed to traffic, and race-car drivers and spectators would arrive from all over the world. The biglietteria was crowded and busy and friends would come to help the family sell tickets and cold drinks from our delicatessen across the street. Huge wooden barrels of ice were lined up outside, filled with bottles of beer, *gazzose* (lemonade) and *spume* (soda).

My little sister Maria, who was very curious, didn't always follow our parents' rules. One day she went too close to the race track and, as the cars came roaring around the curve, she was picked up by the force of the wind and thrown onto the other side of the hill. She flew like a bird and was lucky she didn't get hurt!

On the spot where, in a previous year, one of the race cars had gone off the road and crashed, a beautiful rose garden had been planted, surrounded by a stone wall. This garden was near the school, and my brother Antonio often sat on the wall dangling his legs and waiting. When his friends asked who he was waiting for, he'd answer, "My wife!"

At every birthday, our family sent one another flowers. We also celebrated birthdays with cakes baked at home. The most popular was *la pizza dolce,* a pie filled with homemade cream and chocolate, flavored with *caffè espresso,* red Archemus liqueur, and cocoa cream puffs.

When fall arrived, life at our residence was always very busy with *ricamo e taglio* (embroidery and designing). In the long avenue of tall pine trees, alternating with perfumed oleanders, pine needles and aromatic pinecones full of pignoli nuts fell onto the driveway. We gathered up the pinecones and ate the white pignoli. Then we brought the cones into the house and laid them in the fireplace, where they released a wonderful piney, spicy scent as they burned. That aroma of childhood never leaves my mind: the simple life lived in the name of God each day of our lives, and the cozy feeling of home and family in front of the fireplace, keeping warm and and listening to the stories Mamma read to us.

Another important holiday for us was *Natale* (Christmas). A huge *presepio* (crèche), created to perfection by my talented Mamma, was constructed from large statues, and the grass that represented white snow was cultivated especially for this festivity. Local farmers grew the grass under a cover so that it didn't turn green, but remained pure white. Once the majestic presepio was finished, Mamma warned us children that if we didn't behave, the little Jesus statuette would get up and walk away!

Antonio, who was a little rascal, woke up one morning at 3:00 a.m. and went to block off the manger in the presepio, where the statuette of Jesus was lying, to prevent him from escaping! Antonio also decided to change the lock on the door. He was a clever fellow, always running around. Mamma would chase him, laughing and angry at the same time, because Antonio could be a real handful!

Christmas was so exciting for us! All our Christmas stockings, filled with special little gifts, hung over the fireplace. We would escape from our beds in the middle of the night to peek into the corner of the kitchen, curious to see what our parents were doing. One night, our parents heard us snooping around, our inquisitive faces peering from the staircase. We started to whisper to each other and ask questions. Who brought the presents and goodies? Was it our parents and not *Babbo Natale* (Santa Claus)? Mamma and Papà decided they had to do something to keep the illusion alive for us. They asked a friend to dress up as Babbo Natale, and on Christmas Eve, after we were asleep, they stomped and rattled around the fireplace. Soon Babbo Natale came to visit us in our bedroom! We heard a big deep voice, crying *"Ho ho ho! O bambini! Che buoni bambini!"* (Oh children! What good children!) We were scared, but so excited to meet Babbo Natale in person! Mamma and Papà never admitted to us that this fellow was not the real Babbo Natale.

On the eve of Epiphany, we celebrated *La sei Gennaio* (January 6th). On this evening, we hung our stockings again and waited for *La Befana*, the old woman who flew on her broom and came down the chimney to bring toys and candies to children who had been good all year. If you'd been naughty, you got a lump of coal in your stocking!

The family tradition at our table was bountiful and unforgettable. On Christmas Eve, everything was cooked with the freshest ingredients. Papà would bring home many different kinds of fish, just caught in the Adriatic Sea. Special pots were used to cook the different fishes. Some fish dishes were cooked in the oven, such as *calamari ripieni* (stuffed squid), *gamberoni ripieni al forno* (baked stuffed shrimp), and *merluzzi impanati* (breaded cod) with fresh garlic, parsley, and a little extra virgin olive oil,

All these fish dishes were accompanied by *contorni* (vegetable dishes) of stuffed mushrooms and artichokes, open-face *peperoni* (bell peppers), and *insalate miste* (mixed salads). There were also whole artichokes, looking like big pinecones, with stuffing between their leaves. These were cooked in a large casserole over charcoal, with the cover of the pan also covered with charcoal. *Pesce in brodetto* was a delicious soup made from all kinds of fish, with the addition of fresh tomatoes from the garden. The aroma would reach the sky and send you flying up to heaven when you tasted it!

The local farmers made a special traditional bread with whole wheat and other flours mixed together. This bread was very dense and had large holes in it when cut—always into very thin slices, so crispy and aromatic. The bread was baked in a special oven. In the same oven, the farmers also baked stuffed ravioli. Just to smell the aroma made you want to dance! Once the bread and ravioli were taken out of the oven, it was a tradition for the farmers to climb into the oven while it was still warm. It was supposed to be good for arthritis pain, but I wonder if it was really to breathe in more deeply the aroma of the homemade bread, baked with so much love.

I miss the warm feeling of my family and all the wonderful times we had around our table. Those traditions will never leave my soul until I die.

CHAPTER FIVE

Living Through the War

Once upon a time, I was a little girl with green eyes like the sea and hair blown by the pure breezes of the Italian sky. As the wind blew, the golden sunset was reflected in the windows of my home. The chirping of the birds under the eaves sounded in the distance. I leaned from my bedroom window, touching the branch of a pine tree with my little hands, watching as the swallows dipped and swirled in the dusk.

One terrible day, as I was swinging on the swing under our pine trees in the garden, I suddenly heard terrifying, groaning, wailing sirens filling the air. Seeming to come from everywhere, the sirens were warning us of warplanes coming to drop bombs on us. World War II had broken out. Fire rained from the sky. From then on, those sirens and bombs chased at our heels. With death so near us, we tried to escape without aim or hope of living another day. We cried as we ran like mad and threw ourselves face down on the ground like toy soldiers. Losing our shoes in our haste, our feet were pierced by thorns and pebbles, and at night, we fell asleep in unbearable pain.

During the war, our house was taken over and used as a makeshift hospital to house the badly injured. Wounded people were carried to us on doors removed from our house and used as stretchers. The blood of the wounded was splashed all over the walls, the floor, and the driveway. When the injured patients arrived, we children would run to our well to bring some water, to help revive them. But many times they were already dead. I saw a young dead man whose eyes were still open in his blackened face, frozen like a stone. He looked as if he'd been buried for a long time. Everywhere we looked, we saw death.

We became intimately familiar with death. As young as we were, we saw blood flow in every direction. Mamma wept to see her children witnessing death at such a young age. She was terrified to lose us to the violence of the war. During enemy attacks, people stepped on us and over us as they ran to escape. My sister, Gabriella, would hold onto me and yell, "Don't touch her!" We screamed, terrified, when the bombs shook our home like an earthquake! We hid under our mother's skirt like small chicks without a nest. We hid under the kitchen table or behind the bathroom door. My little sister, Maria, was so scared that as soon as she heard the noise of an airplane she fainted. We had to stop to shake her and wake her up. Maybe she would rather have died than be so scared.

I will never forget how enormous the bombs were that fell from the sky. I put my fingers in my ears but my whole body became shocked and numb from the overpowering blasts. I watched, frozen with terror, as the doors opened in the warplanes and huge bombs plummeted through the air to explode in gigantic bursts of dust and stone, killing innocent people on the spot.

One day, while my brother and sisters and I were running at the sound of the sirens, an enormous bomb fell from a plane and created a tornado of wind and debris that blew Maria, who was only a toddler, off balance. The wind picked her up and threw her over a bridge and into the deep river, where she disappeared under the water. A man who saw it happen spied a bunch of her hair sticking out of the water and was fast enough to grab onto it and pull her out of the freezing river. As he held her small, cold body in his arms, we gazed at her in dread. She looked pale and green, like a little frog, from the cold and dirty water. We thought she was dead, but somehow God made a miracle. Maria suddenly woke up, vomiting water and blood, and she kept on running, following her family. There was no time to cry.

Pain was part of life for us. Everything around us was lifeless and every day death and pain embraced us in a cloud of tears. Step by step we walked on the blood of lost lives in the terrible nonsense of war. Growing up during the war, my young girl's heart cried every moment. I watched people dying of open wounds that poisoned their blood. I saw flies suck the blood from dead bodies, and then swarm after living people to bite them and leave marks on their skin. The eyes of the children of war saw men bicycling without their heads, decapitated by machine guns as they tried to find refuge from the bombs. Our young eyes witnessed flying pieces of bodies all around us.

We ran as fast as we could to avoid being killed and we suffered without water or food for days. When it rained, we drank from puddles, even though sometimes the water was contaminated with insects, frogs, and flies. The color of the water was a rusty yellow. Even if the water was contaminated, we knelt with our tongues sticking out, lapping at it like dogs. The water tasted heavy with blood and metal and dirt. It blew up our stomachs like balloons, but we had no choice. We couldn't turn back. There would be no more smiles from us.

From the distance we heard a sound like an earthquake. After the explosion, two small children ended up on top of the sharp blade of a plow, speared through their delicate bodies. Perhaps they'd been eating, because one of them still held a small spoon in his hand. We saw dead bodies lying in the field, with their tears frozen to their faces and spatters of blood on the ground around them. We had to step over them and keep running.

These horrific images stand vivid in my mind to this day.

One grey afternoon, while I was playing on the swing under the pine trees in our yard, my godmother, Lina, came to visit. As soon as my godmother saw me, she gave me a big kiss and said she was going to Loreto Aprutino to see if there was anything to buy. She asked Mamma if she could bring me—*la commaruccia* (her goddaughter)—along with her. Lina had such lovely naturally curly hair and her beauty shone from within like the rays of the sun. That sun would soon disappear in a lake of blood. Thank God Mamma decided that *la bimba* needed to stay at home with her. She didn't allow me to go with Lina.

The train arrived at our station, and the passengers climbed aboard, including my godmother. The train pulled away. Barely three kilometers into the trip, the train was machine-gunned to the ground, until only dust was left behind. Nobody survived. Over a hundred people died. The odor of burning human flesh could be smelled kilometers away. On the tracks lay pieces of bodies macerated by the bombs. Once more, I could have died. Mamma ran to hug me, crying hysterically from terror and relief that she hadn't let me go on that ride of death. Death has always been part of my life, with every painful breath and in every moment.

One dreadful day, a line of gigantic jeeps with giant wheels came driving up our avenue of pine trees. The jeeps were so enormous that the wheels dug huge pits into the grass. German soldiers carrying rifles arrived with their cannons in front of my family's house. The Germans walked into our home with guns pointed in our faces. They searched the house, finding our food, and took it for themselves. While the Germans occupied our home, they transformed one of our bedrooms into an office filled with radios and electronic instruments. They hid a huge chest containing their instruments of war under our beautiful pine trees. They hid more weapons and electronics in black boxes under the bushes in our garden. The Germans took over all the rooms in our sweet home, leaving us to live on top of one another. Our family of seven people were crowded into one small bedroom, trapped between four walls. There was no place to run. If I only could have flown, I would have escaped.

The only thing left to us was praying to stay alive. The family was starving. The food was taken from our hungry mouths. Papà had hidden our food reserves undergound in our store room, but the Germans found them and took them also. I remember the look of those evil faces, pointing their guns at us, as they searched our house and found our oil, our bread, our cheese. I remember, as if it were yesterday, the shiny leather boots of the soldiers stomping back and forth, with their uniforms so dark and their faces so threatening and harsh! When we peeked at them in their grey uniforms and shining black boots, we felt as though the house itself was trembling.

All seven of us were prisoners in our own house, packed like sardines into one room with the door locked from the outside. When the bombs fell, the bed rocked and we tried to close our ears, keeping our eyes down, staring at the floor. The aroma of hot tea rose up the staircase to our room on the second floor, wafting from our own cauldron over our own fireplace, where the Germans were boiling tea.

At night, the Germans brought in girls off the street and into our kitchen, laughing uproariously and bellowing German songs. Although I didn't understand them, I can still remember some of those German words. While my family were hugging each other tightly in terror of the boisterous soldiers and trembling in fear about our future, the Germans were sipping our boiling tea and swigging our alcohol, shouting and carousing with the women. They were very cruel, and they always looked for more blood. I still hate any shiny boots that recall to me the days of the bloody war. They remind me of the darkest night imaginable, a night that lasted five long years. We could not forget such a painful life. It will remain forever in our childhood's hearts.

But things got even worse. One day—a damned day!—the German Commander, drunk and frightening, began leering at my oldest sister, Adelina. He called to her roughly, "Hey, girl, come here. I want you and I'm going to have you!" He looked mean and cruel, like a blonde devil. It seemed as if he could look right through us into our crowded bedroom. There was no heaven at that time, only hell. The rest of us huddled close to each other, terrified, when the German officer began to chase after my young, innocent sister.

Mamma was standing on the square landing

at the bottom of the steps. My mother, so small and delicate, without even thinking grabbed onto the German Commander's uniform jacket. He dragged her all the way to the top of the staircase and pushed her down. Her legs were bleeding and her skin was lacerated with deep wounds. Horrified, we watched our mother beaten and dragged by the bloodthirsty German officer, as she tried to defend her daughter. She was ready to die for Adelina. Mamma was screaming, "Hide, my daughter! Hide in the closet! Run away as fast as you can!" Mamma's pain and fear were so intense that her throat closed and she couldn't breathe or cry out. We watched this horrendous scene in shock. We screamed and cried, "Mamma, Mamma, help us!" We were terrorized, watching our mother, covered with blood, fall down the staircase, roll backward and land at our feet.

Thank God, just at that terrible moment, Papà walked into the house and saw the unbearable scene. He was horrified! My father became a fury when he saw that his wife had been badly hurt and his daughter almost raped. Blinded by rage, he raised his hand and slapped the Commander twice across the face! My father had violated the law and now *"la fucilazione per tutti noi"* was inevitable. We would be executed by a firing squad against the wall. We were petrified of the pain of an inevitable death and we saw ourselves lined up against a cold wall, waiting to be shot. But where was Adelina? Maybe she had run up to the attic and was hiding there.

As we were screaming in fear, a man who knew my father was passing our house in the distance. He heard the screams and cries from inside. He waited until dark and sneaked into the house to help us escape, like dishrags soaked with tears, one on top of another in the darkest night. While the drunken Germans, snoring like pigs, were sleeping collapsed in a heap with their women, we were able to sneak away from our dear home by the railroad station to our birth town, Loreto Aprutino, where we hoped to be safe at our grandparents' house. We left with nothing, blinded in the dark and numb with fear. God knows there was too much darkness, and the darkness never ended.

We set out on a long journey that seemed to have no end. We had no clothing and no food. I could only cry and cry. I don't know how long our journey to Papagrosso's house took. There were many kilometers to walk, wild brooks to cross and many stops along the way. We had to be careful of land mines, and sometimes mines would explode just after we had passed by. We stopped in stables and huddled next to dirty, smelly pigs to protect ourselves from the cold. We were starving. In the long and hungry mornings, we passed by fruits hanging from trees, and wanted so badly to pick them. But we couldn't eat the fruit because the farmers had coated it with poison so that no one would steal it. The flies buzzing around the fruit were infected; if they bit you, the bite would leave an open sore that wouldn't heal.

I was barely able to walk and was carried most of the way in the tired arms of my father, my brother, and my sisters. I felt a terrible inner fear of dying, and kept crying from desperation. We were so cold, our nails were broken and bleeding and our tender children's feet were pricked by thorns, but we kept going. We cried ourselves into exhaustion from the pain and the tiredness. Sometimes we fell asleep still walking. Near the end of our miserable journey, some merciful people took pity on us and gave us a ride part of the way on their bicycles.

Finally, we arrived in Loreto Aprutino. Papà's sisters and their three children were living at Papagrosso's villa too. When they opened the front door to us, they were shocked, barely recognizing us, utterly exhausted and dressed in old rags as we were. They cried, "Oh my God! Oh my God! What happened?" They brought us inside and wrapped us in blankets. The fire was hot and we gathered around it, shivering. We were worn out and traumatized, but safe for the moment.

On the farm was a little goat named Lisetta. who nourished us with her sweet, warm milk. We drank from her like desperate little birds with our mouths open, lying next to her in the grass. As I held Lisetta and caressed the long fur surrounding her beautiful face, I cried with fear and Lisetta was my only comfort. We were just babies! We held onto her and hung on her, playing with her long fluffy ears. I would grab her neck, climb on her back and ride her. I hugged her tightly and she carried me for a little while longer than the others. My little sister, Maria, was patient and walked, letting me ride Lisetta longer because I was the sickly child.

Pain was an ordinary event during the war and, in addition to my family's struggles, bad accidents happened unexpectedly. One day, my little sister accidentally bumped a long paddle used to stir the boiling animal grease that was used to make soap during the war. Heavens! The boiling soap fell on my mother's legs and burned her skin to the bone, so that she had no choice but to run with her skin cooking, shrieking from unbearable pain at the same time as running for her life! Mamma screamed all night long from the unendurable agony.

Another time, Mamma was suffering from a painful toothache. She finally had a chance to go to a so-called dentist, but who was he? Just a man who said he could take out the rotten tooth. But instead he pulled out the good tooth next to it, leaving Mamma in excruciating pain. The healthy tooth was extracted with no anesthesia, and the bad tooth was left in her mouth. What torture, poor woman! Mamma knew such horrible pain, but she still had incredible strength to survive. She kept her courage because of us, and the love that only a mother could give. Her love was like medicine that nourished us when nothing else could.

Every day was as dark as midnight. When the bombs dropped, we ran for refuge, hiding in a long railroad tunnel that stretched between Loreto Aprutino and Penne. Sometimes we rode Lisetta into the tunnel. Every day, we heard the screams of hungry children. The crowds pushed them aside roughly as men and women tried to hide in the tunnel to save themselves from the bombs. Terrified people stepped on the children to save their own lives. While we ran through the tunnel to escape the bombs, my sister Gabriella protected me, bravely telling the people around us, "Make room. Make room, please. She is suffocating!"

Sometimes I was carried on a little stretcher because I was too weak to run. When the sirens groaned, the bombs would open up the dark grey sky and people would run crying with fear, covered in their own tears. I can still see in my mind's eye desperate children begging for help, while I looked on in pain from my stretcher. Children ran with their noses streaming and their hair covering their eyes. They begged us, *"Un briccolo di pane, per carità!"* (A crumb of bread, for pity's sake!) Mamma told us to divide our bread and give some to the starving children. Everyone was hungry. I saw people pull tufts of grass from the ground and put them in their mouths, wishing and pretending that they were pieces of bread.

Next door to us lived two boys, twin brothers, who had to share what little food their parents could put on the table. One of the brothers ate faster than the other. One day, the slower brother took his fork and stuck it into his brother's nose, so he couldn't eat any more. As the boy screamed with the fork stuck in his nose, his brother took the opportunity to eat as fast as he could. Maybe it was his dream to have a four-course meal! That was what the war did to children. We dreamed about food.

Whatever moved, whether a person or a tiny animal, the Germans shot and killed it. When the sirens blared, we ran *all'impazzata* (at breakneck speed). But where to? There was nowhere to escape from the bombs that fell like huge chunks of hail over our heads. There was no way out and nowhere to go. We were terrified to die in the tunnels, underneath the concrete pavement, where people were crushed to death by rubble.. We were afraid to die as we walked on the road that was covered with human blood. We tried to hide under Mamma's skirt so we couldn't see the blood.

My brother, Antonio, had a little tricycle. Papà made a little wooden wagon which he attached to the back of the tricycle. Every week, we rode in the wagon to the house of a woman who removed the thorns and pebbles from our feet. We screamed as she pulled them out! Even during the war, we children wanted to play, and sometimes Antonio took me and Maria for a ride in the wagon, in the roads around the villa. One time, he told us to get out of the wagon so that he could give a ride to some chickens we saw on the road. He put the chickens into the wagon and off they rode, looking around and enjoying the ride! Maria and I had to wait for our turn to ride in the wagon. Later, when Mamma found out about it, she was angry at Antonio, saying, "What! You left the babies in the street for some chickens?"

Sometimes, between the air raids, children playing outside would find shiny stones and sharp crystals. These stones were shrapnel—the leftover remnants after buildings had been bombarded to the ground. Sometimes they were pieces of bullets or parts of bombs. They might have been explosives. Sometimes they did explode in the children's hands, amputating their fingers.

The war lasted for five long years of unforgettable pain, when people were shot in the back day after day, like mosquitoes. The guns left clouds of smoke under the open sky, which remained grey and smelled of burned flesh and blood for five long years. I remember that Mamma cried for those poor Jewish people who were dying in the Holocaust. She was so compassionate that she felt their pain and suffering along with her own. Mamma said to us, "Charity is the most important thing in life."

The scars from the war remain deep inside, where my heart is still crying for the memories of the childhood I was forced to leave behind.

The Train, 1945

It's been a long time. You came back to me, in your grey uniform.

But you don't want to stay, to open the suitcase soaked with rain.

Because someone is waiting for you on that train.

As you walk toward my door, the tears drop on my floor.

I look at you and I know that you love her more.

You walk so fast to get on that train.

You see only a white handkerchief in the corner of the window, waving goodbye to you.

You quickly turn around, finding the way very hard to come back to me.

Because the rain erased the footsteps, and the suitcase got very heavy.

As I wait for you, I see only the teardrops that shine with the rays of the sun on my floor.

CHAPTER SIX

After the War

After the war, there was nothing but misery. Even if you had money, there was nothing to buy. Italy was devastated. Debris and dust lay everywhere. The land was as grey as the sky and the cold wind blew dust from the crumbled stone and concrete walls over everything: the streets, the animals, the people. All that was left was pain, anger, and wretchedness. The air was contaminated with malaria. Mosquitoes and flies hopped from animals to people, and they bit our tender young skin, leaving scars and marks from the infections.

Death was still all around. A sensitive and emotionally scarred little girl, I was scared, sick, and shocked. My eyes saw death again and again: bodies lying in the street with no arms and no legs, open wounds infected with insects still feeding on the blood. People were dressed in rags, asking for charity, for some food or water. The war made our lives miserable and traumatized us. We still heard the noise of the airplanes, the sounds of machine guns and bombs killing thousands of people with no mercy. We all—little children and adults—still crouched down in terror like frogs at the sounds of airplane and truck motors.

My family went back to the train station in Capelle, where our home used to be. The house's walls and foundation were still standing, but inside the walls were just emptiness and swarms of insects. Terrible smells and splashes of dried blood were everywhere. The only mattress left was full of fleas and bedbugs, and the springs were rusted. We opened up that mattress, painstakingly pulling the wool apart to wash the bugs and dirt away, and laying every piece outside in the sun to dry.

During the war, everything had been stolen from us. Nothing was left of our belongings. The memories of our family were only dust in the wind. Our family of five young children and two adults now faced the grim aftermath of the war: we were starving, without food, without water, without clothing. We slept huddled close together, trying to protect ourselves from the cold and wind. When Papà saw our fingers turning blue from the cold, he blew into our hands to warm them. We tried to keep our spirits up, holding and kissing each other with affection, while we waited for help to come.

The government would give you a voucher, but you had to stand on long lines in the rain and snow until they gave you something: perhaps a loaf of bread, maybe a piece of clothing. Someone told Papà where he could buy some cooking oil *in contrabbando* (on the black market), but that meant paying a large price for a very small amount. Papà was willing to try, and he started walking many kilometers away from home to find the oil. He walked night and day, his feet bleeding and his heart beating out of his chest, but his love for his family was so strong that it made him forget the pain. At home, we waited and prayed for his safe return, dreaming of that magical moment when we would have something to eat. But that precious moment remained only a dream.

We waited by the door every day, hoping forlornly to see our Papà coming in the distance. When he finally returned, he was dismayed to discover that the oil was not edible cooking oil at all, but gasoline—the fuel burned for light in lanterns and to run cars and trucks! We had no choice but to pour that poison into our hungry little mouths. I can still remember the terrible harsh taste in my mouth. We got sick from it and became skinny and weak, like the sparse grass outside our door.

Maria and I were the youngest children. We

used to go outside to play with the leftover colorful metal scraps—red and blue—of the bullets and
bombs strewn in the grass. Dazed and hungry, we
ran around a little, trying to smile and laugh under
the shadow of death. Antonio liked to pick up the
pieces of shrapnel, and he played with other children without knowing the danger of the leftover bits
of metal and bombs. Some of them still exploded
and we were very lucky to survive. Other children
got hurt, losing fingers and hands. The bloody war
never seemed to end and its fear touched our bodies
and souls forever. We could not smile anymore. As
we looked into each other's faces, we saw only terror.

I will always remember my mother crying to
see us suffer. Even though we had a well in front
of our house, after the war the water was thick and
had a sickly, sweet smell. It wasn't safe to drink, so
we had to find water wherever we could and carry it
home on our heads. Mamma always worried about
me, saying, *"Poverina, figlia mia!* (My poor daughter!)
Don't get your hands wet! You'll get sick!"

With no clothes for her family to wear, Mamma had to be creative. She began using leftover
German parachutes to make clothes for us. The
parachute material was stiff, as if it had been
starched. Mamma had no sewing machine and
no thread, so she had to use whatever she could

find to sew the clothes. Sometimes she used yarn or string, making cross-stitches to hold the fabric together. Sometimes she would get thread that was handspun by the peasant women on the farm near our house. She made shirts and dresses with large collars, which we used as hoods to cover our heads when it rained. Through her ingenuity and skill, she was able to exchange handmade clothing for grain to make bread for her family. Mamma also sewed and embroidered sheets and other linens for a *contessa* (countess) who lived across the river.

The head of the family, my hardworking Papà, tried everything to provide food for us. One day, Papà had to deliver to the *contessa* all the embroidered bed sheets that my mother had patiently sewed with her tiny, talented hands. Because the bridge had been bombed, Papà had to wade across the river to deliver the embroidered linens in exchange for grain to make bread, to feed his children's hungry mouths. On his way back, he balanced the heavy load of grain on his head and set off for home, walking all night long under the heavy weight. When he reached the river, he began to wade through the water, carefully balancing the grain to keep it dry, although the currents pushed him and nearly made him fall. Papà crossed the river with the water up to his chin, while holding the load of grain with his hands to steady it.

The family, huddled close to the fireplace, were praying for his safe return home. All at once, the door opened wide and our exhausted Papà burst in, fainting on the floor, as the bag split open and the grain poured out. Ignoring the mess, we ran to gather around our Papà, wailing with fear that he was dead! It was a cold dawn. My father was covered all over with leeches that sucked his blood, although he was so thin and pale that it seemed there wasn't much blood left in his body.

Papà became ill with a high fever, day after day. His body was shaking and covered with blisters. My tiny Mamma attended him night and day, giving him soothing baths of bran. He lay in a huge wooden barrel that served as a tub, his body covered with black pustules. That frightening memory is still vivid in my mind and will never leave me.

Because of all the destruction from the war, there was no plumbing in the houses that were left standing. In the mornings, a big wagon driven by two men came around to all the houses, waiting for people to dump their night's waste into the back. The men would call, "Whatever you have, bring it down!" They emptied the chamber pots into the stinking wagon, and then drove to abandoned fields, where they dumped the waste. All around Capelle, fields that had been lush farmland were now deserted. Nothing grew in the dusty, contaminated earth.

We had no electricity, so we had to use candles to see by in the evening. Often, the wax melted onto the floor, and in the morning we had to scrape the wax off the tiles. We had to iron our clothes with an old-fashioned iron. We put hot coals into the iron to heat it. In order to get the coals going, we had to go outside and swing the iron back and forth. We became so good at it that we started to swing that iron in a circle over our heads! It was exciting to see the dark red coals creating a huge circle in the night sky.

Mamma sewed shoes for us out of rabbit skins, or whatever skins she could find at the neighboring farms. She also wrapped our feet in fabric so that we could go to school. Our school had no heat, no doors, and no desks. The teacher told us to jump up and down like rabbits to keep our feet warm, but the fabric was wet and we still felt freezing. We only had one inkwell with a single pen, for so many little hands to share. The pen and ink were messy to use, and we always ended up with ink on our fingers. Sometimes the inkwell spilled all over us and we returned home with our faces and clothes smudged with ink!

I remember that Mamma sewed special shoes for my First Communion, made from the smoothest rabbit skin. They were so deliciously soft that I felt as if I was flying to visit the angels again. For several days before the ceremony, the little white dress she had made for me hung in our bedroom closet. To me, the dress seemed like a little angel that would help me fly into the sky. I lay in bed with my sisters, dreaming about my dress, until I had to get up and tiptoe to the closet, where I kissed the fabric of my beautiful white gown. It was a sunny day, for once, when I received my First Communion and shared tears of joy with my family. I was given a lot of kisses that day! At least I had one day to live out some of my childhood dreams. There was no peace for us, but only internal pain, present at every moment.

Many people whose homes had been destroyed had to live on the streets, and there was no one to protect the young women from being abused. Almost every night, desperate, bleeding women came to our door. These women had been abused and raped by the German soldiers, who would capture them and take them into their armored tanks, where they raped them. Out in the abandoned farmland, they beat the poor women with shotguns on their heads and bodies and threw them from the top of the hill into the wilderness. These traumatized young women rolled all the way down with their wounded bodies, often fainting at the bottom.

Bruised and bleeding, the women had to climb

back up the steep hill and try to find a road back to a populated area. After walking for hours back to the town, they would knock on doors, looking for refuge. When these poor creatures came to our house and Mamma opened the door, Papa was shocked and tried to keep us away from the doorway to protect us from the terrible sight. The wretched young women looked like ghosts, covered in dirt and blood, starving and wet. They came up the steps of our home screaming in anguish, hitting their heads against the walls until they bled, and pulling their own hair. These desperate women, some of them already pregnant with the enemy, needed a safe place to sleep. My family helped them as much as we could, even when we needed help ourselves. We gave them comfort and a place to stay, in a big storeroom next to the house. There they had to sleep on the bare floor, but at least they were safe. Many of them felt that they couldn't go back to their families with their shame.

Even after the Armistice with the Allies was signed, in September, 1943, the war and the bombing had continued. During this time, a terrible incident happened in our area. The Germans captured a group of men, most likely anti-fascist partisans. The Germans forced them to dig a hole and then executed them right on the spot, in the same hole they had dug as their future grave.

When the American soldiers finally arrived in our region, we were so relieved to see them! They calmed us from our terrible fears, because we felt they were there to liberate us. I remember some young soldiers arriving in their jeep, the wheels bumping up and down on the driveway. They parked on our lawn, bringing us chocolate and cans of fish and meat. They were so young. One of the boys, probably not more than eighteen years old, called our mother "Mamma" and cried to see her because he missed his own mother.

One day, as Maria was playing in the garden, the Americans drove up to our house in their jeep. They were enchanted with her and said, "We're going to take you for a ride!" Before anyone realized it, Maria climbed up into the open jeep and the soldiers drove away with her. The rest of us were upstairs with Mamma, looking out of the window in astonishment! Mamma was beside herself with panic, and started to cry, *"Maria! La bimba! Dio mio, dove sta?"* (Maria! The baby! Oh my God, where is she?) They were gone for nearly an hour. That hour was like a day to us. We didn't know where she could be.

It turned out that the soldiers had taken her to the storeroom where the American army kept all their supplies. They treated her to candies and goodies, and when they finally brought her home, her face was smeared with chocolate. The kind soldiers had stuffed their pockets with goodies for all of us!

Our family was united, and together we put to use our talents as designers and creators of clothing, embroidery, and artisanal crafts, in order to begin a new life and to barter for food. In the mornings, young women would come to learn the art of sewing from Mamma, and in the afternoons, especially on Sundays, the nuns would come for tea. Their prayers and traditions offered a way to rebuild the spiritual life in our family. It took a long time for the railroad to be rebuilt and repaired, as much of the track and many of the train cars had been bombed and machine-gunned. Eventually, Papà was able to return to work.

Little by little the family began to recover, and we children went back to school, like little birds who had lost their feathers. All the past traditions of celebrating holidays, cooking together, praying and going to church were slowly coming back into our lives.

Nightmares visited us frequently. In the middle of the night, a cry of pain and terror would wake us. Sometimes we woke up screaming with fear, like little ghosts. We would run to our parents' room and take refuge in their bed, the only

place we felt safe. Mamma and Papà always comforted us with kisses. When dawn began to lighten
the windows, we heard the little birds beginning to
sing their springtime songs, and we waited for a new
day to come with the sunrise.

To restore our home, we cleaned the house me-
ticulously. After we brought some furniture from our
grandparents' villa in Loreto Aprutino, the house
finally began to look more like a home. We had a
few paintings to hang on the wall, and some chairs
and small tables. We all took turns decorating and
helping Mamma, singing together as we worked. It
was a very good feeling to touch and see the shape
of our home coming back to life.

But we cried to have lost all the family me-
mentos, pictures, books, and photo albums. As we
searched in the corners of our family's memories,
there was nothing there but the ashes of the life we
had left behind.

My Heart

My heart makes me live and makes me die,
Makes me learn how to cry
and smile every day as I feel the pain of joy and love.
I do love my heart
It has the capacity of sense and sensibility.
We keep each other company.
My heartbeat keeps me young
To enjoy the beauty of creation
While the melody of stars
Touches the rainbow,
Embraces the babies,
To follow the dance in the garden of love.
That tender moment takes me where I want to be.
Because my heart speaks to my life.
As I touch the butterfly,
Colors fly from each dot
That shines and sparks with beauty.
That has a special place in my heart.
That gift grows inside of me.
The gift of life: my heart.

CHAPTER SEVEN

Il primo amore: First Love

During my school days, I began to grow into a beautiful, elegant young woman.

One day, I decided not to put on my uniform to go to school. Instead, I wore a blue cotton polka-dot skirt with a white silk blouse, and black shoes. I looked like a schoolgirl in an old black-and-white photo from the past! My shiny brown hair, with short bangs, was plaited into two long braids with blue silk bows at the ends. Freckles dotted my nose and sweet cheeks, decorating my radiant face. I had impish *fossette* (dimples) and beautiful green eyes full of life.

When anyone looked at me, I would blush and turn red like the sweet cherries I loved to taste in the hot summertime at my parents' beach cottage. That day, while I was walking over the bridge and down the path to school, a young seventeen-year-old boy approached me and couldn't keep himself from saying, "Stop, *bella bimba!* I want to talk to you! One day you will be my bride!" When I heard those words, I ran away as fast as I could, my hair flying in the breeze of the spring morning. When I arrived at school, I couldn't stop panting. My teachers wanted to know what had happened, but I was too shy and scared to say anything.

The young man, who was awed by my beauty, waited to talk to me again after school. This time he said, "Don't be worried, little angel. I've just fallen in love with you. I know you have to grow. You are just a baby girl. But one day I will marry you. I will go away to Belgium to make money to give you a home and have children with you."

Another time, this young man, whose name was Carlo, taken by my fresh beauty, exclaimed into the air, "One day, I will kiss that mouth of yours, still smelling of milk, and I will love you with all my passion forever!"

I was only nine years old when Carlo met me. I didn't know anything about love. My parents, especially Papà, were very strict with me and my sisters. Love was taboo for us at that time! When I grew older, Carlo would come to my house every night and stand under my window, serenading me with romantic songs on his accordion. He played that old accordion endlessly, until my sisters and I would fall asleep upstairs in our bedroom, to the sound of his musical serenades.

The memory of that accordion playing under the starry nights is still vivid in my mind. Those passionate notes of a young man's heart in love were beating in every corner of the sky, and finally reached my heart. Forbidden love! In those days, love was forbidden and taboo.

From our second-floor bedroom, I started listening with my heart to the notes of love and I realized that those loving notes from the old accordion were playing just for me. They were keeping me awake, and they even woke up the little birds, tweeting and flapping their wings at the music of love. The golden fireflies of the summer nights blinked around my window, dancing to the notes of my lover! My sisters teased me about *mio amore* (my love) standing all night on his two feet downstairs, playing just for me. I would blush, giggling and shy, and hide my head under my soft lace pillow.

Carlo didn't give up. He showed up every night at the bottom of the staircase to my beautiful home among the pine trees. Carlo's brown eyes were so deeply full of love that when they caught my eyes, I felt as if I were going to faint. I ran away—otherwise my father would kill me!

Papà was annoyed by Carlo's presence and

determination. Every time Papà came down the staircase, he opened the front door of the house and said to Carlo, "What are you doing here? Go home!" Carlo, quickly hiding his beloved musical instrument, made up excuses. "I am waiting for the train!" Papà, irritated, would respond, "The train already passed by!" But Carlo didn't care, and he waited and waited and waited all night long, until 7:00 a.m. He could only exist if he could steal a look at my beautiful face.

After five years of devoted, loving courtship to me, the time arrived when Carlo had to leave for Belgium. The scene of his departure at the train station was like a scene from the film, *Gone with the Wind!* I still remember the moment when Carlo said, *"Arrivederci, amore mio!"* (Goodbye, my love!) He was dressed in a long black coat and his foot was touching one of the lower steps of the train. His was leaning out, stretching as far as he could, to wave his last goodbye to the love of his life: me, *la bella bimba di Papà Fileno.*

Carlo blew me kisses until he nearly suffocated from his tears. The last sight of his handkerchief in the distance stopped my heart. My heart felt cold and my breathing stopped for a moment, leaving me dizzy and faint. My sister ran towards me, trying to prevent me from falling. It was too late!

I woke up on my bed, next to the bouquet of

beautiful red roses that Carlo had left for me before going to the station. There was a note at the side of my bed, saying, "My love, I will be back for you!" Tears of joy and sadness wet my pure white skin, and my tears fell on the roses I was holding tightly to my young adolescent breast.

As soon as Carlo put his foot on land in Belgium, he wrote me a letter. He wrote a letter each and every day, for nine years straight. Each letter would say how much he loved me, how much he wanted to see me, and how much he wanted me to wait for him and be his bride.

In the meantime, I grew more and more beautiful, or so everyone around me said. I broke the hearts of many young men just with my presence at the social dances around town. No man could resist me, for I was well developed, elegant, and sexy. Papà was always in attendance near the door to watch over us, his dear daughters, and he made sure nobody had contact with us.

When we went to Mass, we had to wear veils of black lace to hide our pretty faces. But we were determined to exchange a glance with the boys standing in the back of the church. We would turn, very slowly, to look at the boys through our black lace veils. When I was about eighteen, my father would look at me disapprovingly, folding his arms and telling me, "Don't walk that way!" I didn't know what he meant, and felt mortified. My father would wait for me halfway from church. If any young man said hello to me, I'd tell him to go away! By the time I arrived home, I was red from embarrassment, with my Papà standing there so tall and serious at the doorway.

There were always young men hanging around the train station, and whenever Carlo came back home from Belgium to visit, he would chase them away and start to serenade me nonstop again, every night. I was scared of his never-ending love. I was overwhelmed by his love. I knew that I couldn't kiss him, or there would be a big scandal! Carlo left again without leaving a sign.

On my sixteenth birthday, Mamma gave me a big party. All my friends were invited, including a very handsome young man from another village. He liked me a lot and I liked him. Sometimes when we passed each other in the street, he would ask, *"Permesso, Signorina, posso dire una parola?"* (If you please, Miss, may I say a word?)

As the dance started, we were so excited! Mamma had baked all the fancy pastries, as well as the beautiful cake with sixteen candles. My dress, designed and sewed by my mom, was as green as my eyes, with an embroidered collar, and scallops all around the hem.

The doorbell rang. It was a messenger, come to give us bad news. Riding his beautiful new motorcycle on his way to my house for the birthday party, the polite young man from the neighboring village had been killed in a traffic accident. He was only seventeen. He lost his life coming to see me on this special day. I was shaking. My party, and my sixteen candles, were blown out.

Back in the 1950s, life was great in some ways. It was fun to be serenaded at night under the window. But there were other things that we girls did not appreciate. The young men would wait on the bridge to watch young women go by. There were two gangs that rode motorcyles, and each boy in the gang would "claim" a girl. If anyone else challenged him, the boy would punch him in the nose. Those gangs of young men used to meet on the bridge and fight with brass knuckles over girls, just like in the musical, *West Side Story.*

While Carlo was working in the mines in Belgium, another young man came into my path. Tommaso was tall and handsome, with deep blue eyes and curly black hair. He came from a wealthy family and was very kind. But at that time, and especially in my family, love was prohibited for young teenagers. People would look out of their windows and gossip about us as we walked together in the street. I wanted to be more independent. I had just finished taking a typing course so I could get a job, but Papà wouldn't let his daughters work outside the home. I began to feel stifled. I decided that I needed to leave for America.

In Italy, men would fight over a girl, and I couldn't stand anymore fighting. Every time Carlo came back from Belgium, he would become jealous and want to fight over me. I didn't want to hear people talk. I didn't want to be fought over. I wanted to be in peace and to visit my oldest sister, Adelina, for a little while.

When Carlo found out from my family that I wanted to leave Italy, he immediately came back from Belgium and, on that same bridge where he'd met me for the first time, he told me of his love for the last time. Carlo cried, "Tell me the truth! Tell me it's not true you are leaving for America!" I didn't say a word. I turned my back on him and left him on his knees. He was overcome with anger and hurt. He wept. At that point I stopped. Carlo's tears were streaming down his face. "I love you! I've cherished you since you were a young girl. I wrote to you every day. Where are my letters? Give them back to me!" At these words, I was mortified, and I froze, not knowing how to react.

Carlo exclaimed, "If this is the end and you

really want to leave, go! But remember, one day soon, when you can't find the kind of love I have for you, only then will you understand how much I loved you! And then you are going to suffer without me for the rest of your life!" He ran away like a wounded animal.

That same night, Tommaso, for whom I also had feelings, came to the house to propose to me and to try to stop me from leaving. Nothing would stop me. I had made my decision. In my situation, I had no freedom in life.

Why would I want to leave my country, my family, and my young loves? Maybe I needed some space to reflect. Maybe I needed to see another way of life, and to visit Adelina, who was already living in America, in New Jersey. I was too shy to ask for my parents' advice. Like a fragile butterfly, I flew with my torn wings over the ocean, miles away from my native home, to land on the blooming flowery fields of a vast new country: America.

But I was lost and confused. Torn between the two worlds, without love, without home, I saw only darkness around me. I was ashamed. Without the support of my parents, I felt alone and sad.

Left to Right (back row), Adelina, Nonna, Fileno;
(front row) Grazietta, Emilia

Papagrosso (Antonio)

Papà (Fileno)

Mamma (Lucia)

Our house at the train station in Capelle

My niece Piera in the viale dei pini

My brother Antonio on his bicycle

My brother Antonio and my sister Gabriella

*Left to right: My sister Gabriella, my brother Antonio,
his girlfriend Assunta*

My passport photo

My sister Adelina

My sister Gabriella

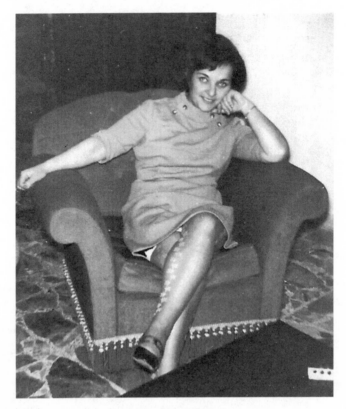

My sister Maria

My brother Antonio, at the back of our delicatessen

Just arrived in America

With Adelina (R) at her house in New Jersey

With Adelina (R) in New Jersey

At home in Rye Brook

Bronxville Furriers advertisement

My fashion show in Scarsdale

At work in the fur business

In Montesilvano, Italy

Bike ride in Montesilvano

Papà and grandchildren

With my friend Lucy at a party

The Package

The package floats between the continents
abandoned below the sea.

They've pushed around the package, to save their own lives
without knowing the pain they have caused others.

But they haven't seen the package, upside-down,
not breathing the air for a moment.

At the shore, the wind blew the sand with the desire of love
to see the grass growing near the concrete wall,
while the child runs to catch the butterfly.

Life has taken a wrong way of painful cruelty,
piercing into the belly of the bleeding heart
stopping to look further to see the stars close to the dream
to light up the street of dark bottomless curves
no exit to life.

Hoping that the stars will shine at least once
in my lifetime.

CHAPTER EIGHT

My Arrival in America

In the days before my departure, it was very hard to say goodbye to my friends. They arrived at my house all dressed up, bringing flowers and gifts. They hugged me, saying, *"Come sei bella, Giovanna!"* (How beautiful you are!) "We will miss you! Always remember your sense of humor. It will carry you a long way."

On the day before my ship was to leave, my family and I took a taxi from our home to Naples, driving for thirteen hours straight. The time felt like nothing. I didn't want to turn my head, to see all the things that I was about to leave behind in my young life. The beautiful city of Naples, with its green pine trees reflected from a distance, stood tall in the light of the dawn. We sat at a café at the Port of Naples, having our last meal together, with cups of espresso, chocolate, and cheese puffs. Everyone, adults and children, enjoyed the wonderful food, but I had no appetite, and couldn't open my mouth from the pain of leaving my family.

I looked at my beautiful family: Mamma, Papà, Antonio with his son Fileno, Gabriella with her two children, and my little sister, Maria. I gazed at them and my heart felt broken into a million pieces. I gave each one of them a piece of my heart when I said goodbye. My mother left me with these words: "Dear Giovanna, our painful tears at your leaving will make the ocean overflow!" As I looked up at the immensity of the sky, I said to myself, "No, I can't leave. Why am I doing this? Because I have to go to find myself and to find my love. I want to see the clear sky and the rainy days, but I will be thinking of you, Mamma."

Mamma tried to persuade me to eat something, but my tears got in the way. I couldn't swallow. I remember the warmth of the soft, rust-colored cashmere coat with a fox-fur collar, which my mother had patiently and lovingly made for me to wear on my trip. I looked at my family one after the other, with the wind whispering a thousand words in my ear. They were there, waiting minute by minute, with their feet up on the step, so as to have the last possible look at me,

The time to leave arrived. Mamma was holding my hand and couldn't let go. I started walking away, but Papà ran after me, kissing me on my forehead and forcing a mint candy into my mouth to give me some sustenance. My mouth was closed. I couldn't breathe. I couldn't talk. I wanted to ask, "Papà! Where am I going? What's going to happen to me?" I can still hear my father crying, *"Mia Giovannella, che Dio ti protegga! Che Dio ti benedica!"* (My little Giovanna, may God protect you! May God bless you!) My heart was broken. I could not even kiss him. I almost said, "I don't want to leave. What will I do without you, Papà?" I took the candy out of my mouth and put it in my pocket to save—my parting gift from Papà.

As the ship to America was departing, I stood on the deck, watching my family still waving goodbye on the dock. Then I closed myself in my cabin and refused to come out. I didn't want to eat or drink. I only wanted to cry. The steward knocked on my door. "Signorina! You must come and have some lunch! Please come out!" But I didn't answer.

When I finally found the courage to go upstairs, a photographer stopped me and asked if he could take a photograph of me. He posted the photo for everyone to look at. My fellow passengers began to give me compliments! How elegant I was! How beautiful! I was shy and embarrassed by the attention, and went back to the safety of my cabin.

It began to snow during the journey. The snow and fog enveloped the ship and the whiteness all around blinded my vision. The cold was freezing my body. I felt as if my heart had stopped beating. I didn't know where I was and I didn't know where my heart was. I felt even colder at the thought that I had left my family and my home. Now I couldn't remember why I had wanted to leave.

After many days of sailing between the sky and the sea, I arrived—much thinner and pale with fear—at the misty Port of New York, in my fancy cashmere coat with its silk lining and fox-fur collar, my high heels, and my shiny brown hair blown by the wind. As we drew into the port, I peered in front of me and the first thing I saw was the Statue of Liberty, so dazzling in the distance, tinted by the misty weather. The grey sky was filled with white seagulls flying toward my ship in a welcome dance. Cold chills went down my spine. I lost my balance, my heart beat faster and faster, and I said to myself, "I wish that my ship would turn around and sail back to Italy! I am scared!"

I was the last passenger to step off the ship and to touch the land of America. The warm, welcoming voice of my sister Adelina, calling me sweetly, woke me from my nightmarish daydream. My cold sweats stopped for an instant. A smile spread on my face and my heart warmed up when I saw my beautiful sister waving to me in the distance. I ran into her arms, crying from happiness to be with each other again after so many years. My sister's beautiful face brought me back to my childhood memories: the tears, the kisses, the endless embraces. Adelina touched my face and my hair, observing the elegant coat I wore, and showered me with sweet compliments. As we walked, she put into my mouth delectable confections she had baked for me.

It was a long drive to Adelina's house in New Jersey, but we had plenty to talk about on the way. When we left the highway and drove along residential streets, I gazed around in amazement, saying, "Look, Adelina! Those houses look like pictures in a magazine!" The fancy houses were surrounded with beds of flowers.

In my family, it was a tradition to prepare a meal of delicious *tortellini* each time someone arrived or left for a trip. I felt the *acqualina in bocca* (my mouth began to water) at the thought of the tortellini melting in my mouth once I arrived at Adelina's house. Finally, I felt hungry! When we arrived at Adelina's home in New Jersey that evening, I was overjoyed to see that she had prepared a beautiful dinner of tortellini. I looked around, admiring the elegant table set with flowers and fancy china. The bedroom that she had readied for me was decorated in pastel colors, and the sheets were embroidered with lace. The pillow I slept on was the softest silk. On the night table, which was covered with silk cloth, an oriental lamp illuminated my photo.

Since I had arrived in New York, even though I was with my sister, I missed my family all day long. There was nowhere to go. We went outside to play in the snow! Adelina's friend Beverly would always stop by. When visitors came to the house, the conversation was in English. I didn't understand it, but I tried to smile and look pleasant.

Soon, packages began to pile up in front of our door. In those packages were gifts from my dear parents, sent all the way from Italy. While I was opening the gifts, I was on top of the world. At the same time, I felt sad because all the rest of my family were far away overseas. Inside the packages, packed and sent with so much care, were beautiful handmade dresses, Italian shoes *alla moda* (in style), and fancy purses ready to be worn on outings. When I wore these beautiful clothes, I instantly became the royal queen that others said I had always been. I had style and elegance! When I walked down the street, people would call after me, "Hey, Barbie doll!" One day, two women from a shop stopped me, carrying a little package. They said, "You are so elegant!

Every morning, we look through the shop window to see what you are wearing. Here, we've brought some lace for you!"

Inside the packages from Italy were also letters. Mamma would always include a freshly cut tea rose in each of her letters. "My dear daughter, it's five o'clock in the morning. I am sitting in the corner of our beautiful garden with the fresh rosebuds in my hands. They are wet with *rugiada* (dew) like your mother's tears. I kiss them as if I am kissing you, my child, with all my heart and my loving thoughts. I miss you, we miss you so!" As I read these letters, tears ran down my cheeks, joining over many miles' distance Mamma's overflowing tears. She used to say, *"Il mare è ingrossato dalle nostre lacrime!"* (Our tears are making the ocean deeper!)

Every so often, Adelina and I would decide to call our parents in Italy. At that time, it was a big affair to call overseas. We had to make a reservation with the operator at least a month before the call. Then we wrote to Mamma and told her when we'd be calling. To take the call, she had to go to the Centralino, which was a public switchboard office in the town.

When the call went through, the reception was terrible! As soon as the line opened between the two countries, we heard a rhythmic, roaring sound, like ocean waves. We'd yell, "Mamma, Mamma!" and she'd yell back, *"Figlia, figlia mia!"* (My daughter!) And then, all too soon, the receiver went dead and our call ended.

One day, as I was looking out the window at all the big cars, I saw one of them pull into our driveway. It was special delivery, bringing me a package from home. Inside, I found a book, handmade by my Mamma, titled *My Little One Far Away From Home.* Mamma had written a story about a girl who was lost in an unknown country, miles and miles from her home. Mamma said in this book, "Don't forget these words, Giovanna! Even if you lose your Mamma, her heart will accompany you now and forever. With my silver rosary beads in my hands, I know that God will always guide you with my prayers, and God will give you the strength to face any obstacle in this big new world!" I lived by these words, and I found strength and peace in my mother's love and poetry.

I was a sweet and fragile young woman, just arrived in America, with a suitcase in my hand, a trunk filled with memories and gifts, and big dreams in my heart. I was sensitive and kind. I loved making people happy and I had a strong sense of humor that has never left my soul to this day. I loved making people laugh!

I had planned to stay at Adelina's home for six months, on a tourist visa. But Adelina wasn't happy in her life, and she needed my support. She asked me to stay longer. I never expected to stay for years.

During most of my visit, I stayed at home with Adelina, whom I really adored. One winter day, we both dressed up in fancy clothes and went to visit New York City—my first time going out on the town in Manhattan. The occasion was a fancy ball at a private club. The ballroom seemed filled with young Italian men, and that night, destiny brought into my path the man who would become my future husband. A young, handsome, elegant man crossed the room and reached for my hand. As the melody of "Autumn Leaves" began to play, he asked me to join him on the dance floor.

I was gradually becoming more outgoing, though my innocent nature turned my cheeks bright red, like freshly picked cherries. But I had no time to say no. I was swept onto the dance floor in a romantic embrace—by a great dancer! Those expert feet propelled us around and around, and soon we young souls were flying around the dance floor like butterflies, beautiful and free. We danced all night long, lost in a loving courtship. It didn't take long for Rino to ask my sister Adelina for my address, so that he could visit me in New Jersey after the soirée.

After only a few visits, Rino asked for my hand in marriage. His proposal took me by surprise, and put me in even greater conflict. Now I had a more difficult choice to make. I liked Rino, but I wasn't in love. I was afraid of the unknown, but I tried to convince myself. I promised myself, "I'll be okay. After all, now I'll be able to have a baby and a family. My dream is to be a mother. That's all I ask of God!" With these hopeful prayers and wishful thoughts, I went outside onto the terrace in my elegant pink silk dress. With the dream of a future family in my heart, I put my arms around Rino's waist and let him kiss me. He whispered in my ear, "Would you marry me?" Still unsure, I told him I had to ask my sister first.

I asked Adelina, "What should I do? Should I stay or should I go back to Italy?" I told her that I wasn't in love with Rino. But Adelina pleaded with me, "Stay with me. Don't go back!"

The wedding was scheduled for December 17th. As soon as the date was chosen, a big brouhaha exploded. My future mother-in-law stepped in and said, "That day will bring bad luck!" In Italy, the number seventeen is considered unlucky, and she was a superstitious woman. Adelina took matters into her hands and made the final decision for us. She told us, "The seventeenth is a beautiful day.

It will be my birthday that day, so let's celebrate life and special times! The wedding will happen that day no matter what." It was easy for her to decide that for us! *Era nata con la camicia!* (She was born with a silver spoon in her mouth!)

The wedding day arrived. It seemed that the disaster my future mother-in-law had predicted was going to happen. There was a terrible snowstorm! Snow and ice covered the streets. All the windows were frozen shut with icicles. On the way from Port Chester, in Westchester County, New York, to the church in New Jersey, the cars carrying the groom, the best man, and the bridesmaids broke down like little paper toys. The wind blew the snow into a tornado in the deserted streets.

That morning, at my sister's house, I woke up with a fever and a bad sore on my lip, but I managed to get out of bed so that the show could go on. A beautiful lace wedding gown covered with pearls— an original creation by Alfredo Angelo Designs— was hanging on my closet door, ready to be put on. The train was long and very fancy, and the dress was white as snow, like the purity of my young heart. But the whiteness of the snowstorm outside my window was more blinding than my white wedding gown. Adelina helped me dress, and then, wearing my fine clothes, I opened the door and stepped out into the snow. But the front step was slippery and I was taken by surprise. Down I went, in my exquisite gown, scraping my knee on the icy flagstones. Shaken and mortified, I somehow made it to the car.

At the church, I tried to smile, but I felt strange. I looked at my reflection in the mirror, wearing my beautiful white gown. A delicate white veil framed my face with droplets of pearls. I appeared to my eyes like a princess in bare feet, or a fresh rare lily flower floating on a lake of sadness. My sadness clouded everything, and it echoed like a mournful song in the empty church, as I walked slowly down the aisle. The pews were empty and the church was cold. Tears of sadness and fear fell from my fresh young face onto the stone floor of the church. In a daze, I kept my straight, regal posture and continued walking to the music of the piano.

I desperately wanted to find a friendly face. There were only three people in the church. The pianist abrubtly stopped playing the wedding march. I looked around and realized no one from the wedding party was there yet. The silence was so complete that I could hear the snow and ice tapping against the stained glass windows. I could hear my own breath. All at once, a door opened at the entrance to the church and my future husband appeared, as handsome as he could be. The beautiful bridesmaids and the best man followed. The wedding march began again.

The ceremony was over quickly. Then I learned of my new husband's state of affairs. The young groom was so broke that when it was time to tip the priest, he had to ask the best man for ten dollars. After the wedding ceremony, we went to the reception hall, where there was a lovely dinner ready for us. I danced with my new husband, but it was not the same as the night we had met. I felt a sense of dread.

When the reception was over, I discovered that my husband and I couldn't go home because he had no money to pay for the dinner. The gifts of money we'd received from the guests were not enough to pay for everything. I was in shock. I didn't know anything about my husband's financial distress.

We had to sit at the table for hours, I with my head in my hands. Under the table, my feet slipped out of my shoes, and as I looked around at the empty tables in the empty room, I felt as if I were lost, barefoot, in the winter storm. It was cold both inside and outside my heart. I thought I would have to wash dishes to pay for the dinner. My husband's brother had asked to borrow his car to bring his girlfriend home. We were stranded. We stayed seated, unspeaking, until 3:00 a.m., when Adelina returned in answer to my desperate phone call.

Adelina saved us, and ended up paying for the entire reception. My husband had no car to transport me, so I went to my sister's house, while he made his way back to his family's home in Port Chester. We spent our wedding night in separate houses, in different towns. I felt numb, as if someone had hit me over the head. I was isolated from the world.

I stayed with my sister for two more weeks, growing more and more mortified and embarrassed. Adelina finally called my husband, reminding him angrily that now he had a wife to take care of. I was shipped like an unwanted package to my husband. He had rented a one-bedroom apartment on Williams Street in Port Chester. When I arrived with Adelina at the apartment, there was no furniture, no food—nothing, just cold, bare walls. As a young bride, my dreams disintegrated into nothingness from the cruel reality of poverty and despair.

I didn't complain. I thought this was normal for everyone in this strange country. I got busy cooking and cleaning, the way I had learned from my Mamma. I started to make the house into a home, creating *profumo di casa mia* (the scent of my home). Adelina felt compassion for me and brought whatever she could. She tried to make sure that I was taken care of as I always had been.

Not many weeks went by before my husband's

father suggested that I should go to work. These were words I didn't want to hear. I was still trying to orient myself. I didn't know the language. I didn't know the man I'd married, or the country I lived in now. But my husband didn't hesitate to agree to his father's proposal. He brought me, his young bride, to one of the worst areas in Port Chester: the sweatshops. In a dreary factory, under miserable conditions, I did piece work, sewing clothes along with many other women. The rule was: if you didn't work, you didn't get paid. It was hot and airless, and the constant noise of the rows of sewing machines was overpowering and exhausting.

My lovely dream—to have children, to be a homemaker, to be a charming hostess, and to make beautiful dresses for my future children—crumbled like a sand castle under the winds of a dark storm. A new chapter started in my miserable life. I burst into tears when I was alone, but I never complained to my husband or shared my inner feelings and pain.

What a shock for me, who had always lived under that crystal bell jar, cherished and protected by my family because of my fragile health! Now that crystal bell jar dissolved into the immensity of nothingness. I was lonely, lost, and trapped in a life that I never expected to live. No love, no understanding, no rest. No time to exist as a woman.

I didn't know how to claim my right to be a woman and a wife, to enjoy one day of rest a week without having the pressure to work. I looked for one word, one gesture so as not to feel alone. I thought this must be normal for every woman, that after marriage she had to sacrifice her life.

The Immigrant

To run, to have no destination, dangerous emigration
without future,
world completely different, without tomorrow,
without true resources, with sadness, lost far away from my
family,
on deserted routes.

To run, to arrive on time without asking where I am, what I do.

I don't understand a word!

I walk fast to arrive home, I climb the staircase,
the staircase leads me to that door already closed.

I put my hand in the mailbox with my heart in my throat.

I am looking forward to a written note, a blowing kiss in the
wind, a comforting word from my parents,
But the mailbox has no bottom, so whatever note has been
written has flown away, back again with the wind of
overseas between the two worlds!

I cover my face with my hands to hide the teardrops that fall
and wet my dress,
tears of a lost young girl who with such courage
looks at the future

to touch the hopes that surround the path of life!

CHAPTER NINE

The Sweatshops

When I started working in the sweatshops, abuse and suffering became part of my everyday life. Working in the sweatshops was a very demeaning job. I, a young bride—such a tender, beautiful girl—saw my dream of happiness and family broken into a million pieces, like a shattered crystal champagne glass.

After work, I spent the evenings alone, without my husband, who was working night-shift jobs. I couldn't sleep, I couldn't breathe, I couldn't sustain such a tormenting, abusive life. I scrubbed our clothes in the bathtub because no one told me that there was a laundry room with washing machines. Late at night, in our small, ugly kitchen, I cooked an exquisite dinner for my husband and set an elegant table with a linen tablecloth. I cooked everything from scratch, and waited until 3:00 a.m. for my husband to return. When he finally came home, he would ask me if I had already eaten. I always said I had, but I was lying. I didn't eat because I wanted to die. I couldn't face another day in the sweatshop. I was too delicate and fragile. I was very shy, and when strangers looked at me I started to cry.

All night long, the interminable noise of those sewing machines from the sweatshop hammered in my ears. It tortured my mind all day long, and at night it prevented me from sleeping. All through the night, as I tried to sleep, I felt the room shaking, but it was my own body trembling. The ticking of the clock was like torture in my brain. I counted every second until I had to get up and go to work. Morning came and I didn't have the energy to crawl out of bed. I was exhausted by the sleepless nights. When I woke from my uneasy sleep, I heard the church bells ringing. I stopped for a moment, surprised, because inside my head, I heard my Mamma's voice, *"Fai la buona, bimba mia. Sei tanto saggia. Da lontano ti proteggerò."* (Do your best, my child. You are so wise. I will protect you from afar.)

I had no strength and dressed myself in a lifeless, mechanical routine. I sat on my bed every morning, rocking myself and calling, "Mamma, Mamma. Help me, Mamma! I am waiting for you every night, Mamma. I remember when you kissed my forehead, and your sweet hands caressed my hair, to take away the pain from your little girl. Your maternal love nourished my heart, while I was waiting for more. It was so beautiful then, Mamma. Time will never erase the beauty of your touch and your love. That will always be with me. I have only painful memories now, without you, Mamma! I am sending you these words of love, because only you, Mamma, can understand what life has been without you."

I felt lost. I didn't know where to go, I didn't know the language, I didn't know anyone around me. I didn't know if I could manage to walk to work because I had no strength in my thin, weak legs. I was physically and emotionally drained by the hours and hours of endless work.

As I dragged myself to the sweatshop, I was too dazed to be aware of anything around me. My eyes could only see the dark walls along my route. My vision was blurred with exhaustion, and tears filled my eyes every moment of my workday. Those dark walls reminded me of the concrete walls where people were executed by firing squads during the war. Those terrible images never left my memory.

I never noticed any trees or flowers. I walked with my head down, and never saw the beautfiul young man standing on the corner waiting for me. One day, he stopped me as I stumbled along the sidewalk, and asked, "Don't you see me? For three years, I have been waiting here to see your beautiful face every morning. You are so beautiful! Where are you going?" I responded, "I am going to work. Go away, go away. I am married!" The man said, "How is it possible? You can't be married! If you were my wife you wouldn't go to work!" Tears trailed down my cheeks as I looked at the kind, sweet face of that handsome man with red hair and blue eyes. I still see his face vividly in long-ago memories, a reminder of the lost life that I never had, and still dream of.

When I felt desperate, I screamed for Mamma as loud as I could! Sometimes I had to walk through rain, snow, or hail on my way to work. Without a raincoat, I would arrive at the sweatshop soaking wet and trembling from the cold. At the end of the day, I came home shivering with pneumonia. I would wail, "Mamma, help me! Please help me!" In my imagination, I was running and running towards my mother, throwing off my shoes to run faster and faster to reach her, waiting for me at my doorstep. I would see her in front of me, but it was just an illusion. My mother was not there to embrace me, her little girl. My mother was miles and miles away across the ocean. I would sit on the fire escape, trying to breathe. As I looked around, no one was there. Empty space, empty room.

The wind was so cold against my face in the

freezing early mornings of winter. Without gloves, without boots, that freezing cold was all around me—the freezing cold that comes from emptiness and the lack of love and care. Sometimes, running through the snowy streets, I ran right out of my shoes and arrived barefoot. I had to be on time to punch the time card. I was afraid to be late! I cried on the way to work because I knew that if I was even one minute late, they would take half an hour off my paycheck, which was only eighteen dollars a week to begin with. In the face of the wind, I grabbed my umbrella and leaned against the gale so that I wouldn't blow away. The umbrella turned inside out and I pulled it down with all my weight, trying not to fly like Mary Poppins up into the sky! At least my sense of humor never deserted me. I smiled at the image, although my heart ached. I wanted to live. I wanted to dream of everything that could be mine. Maybe it would be better to fly away from the painful reality of my life.

My only refuge from the cold and despair was a church I passed on the way to work. My feet were frozen by the ice and I could barely walk. My shoes would stick to the ground and I had to pull and pull them until I fell and hit my head against the frozen path. With a bleeding cut on my head, I still found the energy to go into the church, to kneel and pray. Before going back out to the street, I pulled up my girdle and stockings and tried to ready myself to confront the cold again. I couldn't believe that my destiny held so much pain. When would I be free, light-hearted, able to feel joy again? Now, I was too exhausted even to take a walk in the park. Why should I pray all the time without having a taste of the beautiful life, a pinch of pleasure or a desired kiss!

I was so shocked by my dull, painful life in the sweatshop that the only things I knew were pain, hard work, and those concrete walls surrounding me as I walked to the sweatshop. Such a fragile young woman couldn't handle the absence of love, the empty marriage, no family, nothing but work all day long. Without knowing the language, I couldn't communicate. I tried to smile but I only wanted to cry. Sometimes when I got home, I would play Claudio Villa singing, *"Mamma, solo per te la mia canzone vola! Mamma, sarai con me, tu non sarai più sola!"* (Mamma, only for you my song is flying! Mamma, you'll be with me, you won't be alone anymore!) I listened to the sweet music and cried and cried. It was a relief to cry.

My experience of life had become like trying to climb slippery concrete walls all the way up to the top. Looking at them from a distance, those walls seemed impossible to climb. But here I was, attaching myself to these oily, slippery walls, with my torn wings and failing strength. I tried to climb but there was nothing to grab onto. I couldn't do it and yet I had no choice. I must do it! I tried to climb high, with my heart in my throat, without giving up. But as soon as I thought I'd reached the top, I slipped all the way down again. I stood up and tried again, struggling and crying. I implored and prayed. I wanted my mother, then my father. I tried, with strong faith and hope of a better future, to climb up again.

I was working so hard and such long hours that many times I felt weak to the point of fainting while still stepping on the sewing machine pedal. Sometimes the machine sewed right over my fingers, breaking my nails and making my fingers bleed. I can still see the scars. The foreman brought me to the hospital to pull the painful needles out of my nails, and then I had to go right back to work. Sometimes when I fainted, I made a sighing sound, so that the other women thought I was singing. They suspected that I might be pregnant, but the truth was that I was getting sicker and sicker.

I decided not to eat. I wished that I could die and not go to work anymore. I hid behind a door at lunch time. The other women invited me to eat lunch with them but I wouldn't answer. Even when my husband occasionally brought me a small sandwich, I waited for him to leave and then threw it in the garbage. Why eat? I wanted to die.

At night, I had terrible nightmares and began to sleepwalk, trying to escape from the misery of the sweatshop. In my sleep, I packed a suitcase and dressed myself, ready to escape. I was running away from the sweatshop, and in my sleep I finally walked into the wall. I hit my head against the wall of my living room and woke myself up. Then I held my head in my arms, crying from despair. When my husband came back from work, he found me, confused and desperate, leaning against the wall. He said, "Where are you, Gio? Gio?" I didn't respond. I was dying inside.

I became weak and anemic. Before I knew it, I ended up in the hospital. I was so sick that I didn't have the energy for anything beyond survival. I had no one to tell. I was too embarrassed to tell my sister, Adelina. I lost so much weight that I weighed only ninety pounds. I could barely stand on my feet anymore. One day, my mother-in-law walked into the house. I was washing the dishes. She asked, "Who is that girl over there?" My husband answered, "That's Giovanna." My own mother-in-law didn't recognize me because I was so thin and pale. My husband became frightened. He decided to send me back to my family in Italy to recover. He went to the bank and took out some money, saying, "Go to Italy and get better!" I was only twenty-seven years old. I was longing to see the familiar faces of my family. Maybe they would comfort me.

GIOVANNA MARIA ACCIAVATTI

To Italy and Back Again

*A*fter just three years of marriage, I arrived in Naples on a ship from New York, looking like an emaciated ghost. I was wearing my red coat with silk polka-dot lining. My dress matched the colors of the coat and my white gloves were edged with soft fur. I waved from the ship and my beautiful, loving family were there, so impatient to touch me, to kiss me, and to comfort that fragile butterfly with her torn wings. Without my family, I would have fallen from the sky, unable to survive.

I will never forget the moment when I rejoined my family, or the image of my Mamma in her stylish coat, stretching her hand to wave to me from across the ship. My brother Antonio ran to me, lifted me up in his arms, and hugged me tightly. Crying, he said, "What did they do to you, my *principessa?* Is there anything left inside this coat?" I was trembling like a little girl, finally living the moment I had been dreaming about.

The taxi that was waiting for me was full of *panini all'abbruzzese* (sandwiches in Abruzzo style): cheese puffs, panini with prosciutto, with porchetta, with frittata, with chocolates, with Baci Perugina. We stopped at the first café on the way home. *"Ecco il cappucino! Che vuoi? Mangia qualchecosa!"* (Here's a cappucino! What do you want? Eat something!) My family filled my mouth with all these delicious tastes to try to restore my body and my soul. I rested and slept. All I could think about was that tomorrow the bell would not ring at the factory for me, and I wouldn't have to listen to the noise of the sewing machines, that sounded like the sirens from the war.

I stayed with my family in Italy for six months and was taken care of like a queen. I was served breakfast and lunch in bed, and the doctors came to the house to treat me. My family was afraid to let my friends see how ill I looked. My eyes stood out in my face, and I looked terrified of life.

The house was filled with fresh flowers, which restored my soul. My family asked me, "Giovanna, how is America? Are there flowers, trees, nature?" I answered, "Oh, no! It's all concrete walls, all around." They asked again, "America is really like that? Are there only concrete walls?" I said, "Yes, there are only concrete walls. That's what I see every morning!" Again, they insisted, "So, America is just concrete? Is it ugly?" I repeated, "Yes, just concrete walls. That's all it is!" The family took my words to be the truth.

Later, when Maria visited me in America, she was astounded to find that there were beautiful trees and flowers after all. She cried, *"Giovanna! Guarda i fiori!"* (Look at the flowers!) I was just as surprised as she was, because until then, I had never noticed them. Maria opened my eyes!

My stay in Italy was wonderful. I began to recover and to feel like a young woman again. Because my father's job with the railroad allowed my family to travel for free, Maria and I went on a trip to Loreto delle Marche, where the *Santa Casa della Vergine Maria* (Holy House of the Virgin Mary) stands.

Ever since I was a little girl, I have always dressed elegantly and walked with a sophisticated step. Elegant comportment has always been my advantage. For the bus ride, I put on a pair of pants and some makeup. But people looked at me strangely. In Italy in the 1960s, women didn't wear pants! I was ahead of the fashion. On the bus trip, I was captivated by the beauty of a handsome young man, blond with blue eyes and white teeth. He fell in love with me right away. Love at first sight! This beautiful young man was playing a little tune of love on his guitar as the bus wound around the mountain roads.

When we returned from the trip, he began to court me with a variety of gifts. He came to my home every day. He knew my father because they worked for the same company. Papà didn't like him and kept saying, "What are you doing, coming around here?" Papà could tell that something was cooking! But I liked the young man very much. He was charming and funny. He brought me and my sister to the beach to dance and listen to music. We talked about life and we laughed together. I enjoyed our conversations, and was able to leave the bad times behind for a little while. I felt as if I were reliving my younger life, for a moment that could last forever. But after a while, my father decided it was time for me—a married woman—to go back to America. That for me was hell.

In Italy, in the early 1960s, many things were taboo. Women couldn't talk about their personal feelings and intimate lives. For this reason, I didn't have the courage to tell my family how unhappy I was in my marriage. I couldn't tell them that I was no wife, no mother, but just a slave, working nonstop like a beast at the sweatshop. I sadly put my head down in submission and went back to America, even if, deep down, I wanted to stay in Italy. I wanted to have a taste of life, to look for love, to walk on the beach with the wind blowing my hair and the passion of music under the stars.

I will never forget those blue eyes and that white shining smile of my lost love, who begged me to stay and marry him. It wasn't possible. At that time in Italy, divorce was prohibited. I wished Mamma had realized how miserable I was and said to me, "Stay here with me." But she didn't.

The fragile little butterfly flew again from the waters of the Mediterranean over the Atlantic Ocean, hoping to land with her restored wings, mended by her family's love, in a better place. That sky was so beautiful, but not for me.

When I was leaving to go back to America, my love had cried for me, holding me and telling me not to go. After I left, he fell sick and ended up in the hospital. One day, I received some recordings in the mail, with a note from him. "Listen to this music and think of all our evenings spent together, walking along the beach and listening to those musical notes of love in the summer breeze. In the summertime the wind brought my whispering words of love to your ears. Those notes are caressing your face, your lips, your beautiful hair!"

Full of love inside my soul, I returned from Italy with a dream in my heart: to cradle a newborn baby in my arms with tenderness. I felt an endless love, daydreaming with open eyes. I imagined a bud in a garden of flowers, embroidered with a golden thread. It was so small in my arms, and I sang a lullaby to the little bud. In my imagination, I danced. I felt I was in paradise. In that magical moment the thread became brighter and brighter. This was my constant daydream.

At night, I started to embroider delicate little newborn outfits, so elegant and sweet. If the doctor had told me that I was pregnant, I would nearly have died of joy! But that never happened. I was alone. I had to face the harsh world all by myself. I felt that I deserved pain and such punishment. My only comfort was my mother's prayers, memorized as a child while going to church.

Reality was different, and when I came back from Italy, the shadow of my pain followed me everywhere. I went back to work, not only in different sweatshops but also at many other jobs. Altogether, I endured nineteen different jobs. Many times, I had to leave these jobs because the boss made a pass at me. I went home and didn't go back.

How could I, a shy, delicate, sophisticated woman, again face such mental and physical torture? I don't know how I survived. But every time I fell, I got up again. Every time I lost a job, every time I got sick, every time I had an accident, I always kept the hope of seeing the sun shining in my heart, and the smile of a child, and flowers blooming. I held in my mind the image of a child playing nearby in a kitchen garden, while I was setting the table with delicious food. My child and I would joke together about why the cat was looking at us and playing with a ball of yarn.

Every day, for five years, I worked at different jobs in different factories. I felt hopeless and trapped. But one day, a woman friend asked on my behalf if I could work at a cushion factory as an apprentice, to learn the trade. At the time, I still didn't know much English. The owner was a tall, thin Jewish man named Michael. God bless him, where ever he is. He was kind to me. He would say to his assistant, "She can't speak English, but she communicates with her eyes."

I was a quick learner and I soon began earning a paycheck. It was always small—only twenty dollars a week, but that was good money in those days. It was enough to buy some food and a few other necessities. I became friends with Michael and his family, which was a great experience for me. He invited me to every big occasion, to parties and bar mitzvahs. During the ceremony, I would hold the Torah upside down, since I couldn't read the Hebrew. Michael would come over and turn it the right way, saying, "It's better like this!" I'd laugh to myself, "What did you do that for? It's all the same to me!"

After that job, I worked in other factories. I took a job in an eyeglass factory, where my health began to suffer. I had to use a cutting wheel to cut the glass lenses, but no protective mask was provided. I had trouble breathing from the toxic fumes. My lungs got worse and I felt overstressed from having to produce so many pieces.

Even when I worked at factory jobs, I always dressed in a sophisticated manner. At the eyeglass factory, the boss always complimented me, saying that I didn't belong there. One day, the manager noticed me, and my boss said I should go with him to his office. The manager asked me to take a better job at a different location. I became a technician. I was now a specialist, putting together detailed pieces of instrumentation for airplane pilots' compasses. This was a real challenge, but I enjoyed challenges and I loved to use my imagination at work. The new factory was on Long Island, so my husband and I rented a house there from a well-to-do family. During the day, I worked for the family in their house, and at night I worked in the factory.

While I was in America, Mamma said to Antonio, "Take me to see the nuns, I want to see them before I die." They drove to Teramo, but the convent was empty. They went inside anyway, and Mamma started to kneel at the altar to pray. But she slipped down onto the floor and lay on the cold stones. Finally, she stood up again, and began to point out where everything had been in the convent. Looking around, she said, "Antonio, over there was the theatre! Over there was the school. That's where we slept! How wonderful to see it all again. Thank you for letting me relive some of my childhood memories."

Not long afterwards, on a hot summer day in August, I received an unexpected phone call from Italy, telling me of the death of my dear mother, Lucia. She died young, in her early sixties. When I heard the terrible news, I had a sudden nervous breakdown. The pain left a gaping hole in my heart.

What a tragedy for my family! Adelina and I immediately flew to Italy to be at our mother's funeral. When we arrived, the funeral procession had already begun. Dressed all in black, we walked four long kilometers under the burning hot summer sun, to the cemetery of Loreto Aprutino. Our family was destroyed by the incomprehensible loss of such a beautiful soul and loving mother. Mamma had these words carved on her headstone: "I rejoiced when God called me to Him!" But for us, the tears were bitter.

We were silent on the way back to the airport

in Rome. When we said goodbye to our Papà and sister Maria, the atmosphere was cold and tense, like a military farewell. Adelina and I sat under the rain in our wet black dresses, crying endlessly, our tears joining the falling rain. We must have looked poor and destitute, huddled in our black clothing. People passing by us gave us coins for charity.

When we landed at Kennedy Airport in New York, four beautiful children and a husband were waiting for Adelina, and she went back to her happy life.

I went back to the house in Long Island. Now I felt even worse than before. I was more lost and alone. No more of those caring letters from Mamma would arrive in the mail for me, carrying freshly cut fragant roses from her lovely garden and her warm, loving words of comfort. I looked hopelessly at the mailman every day, as if I believed my mother was still alive, sending me messages from overseas. I tried to comfort myself with the thought that Mamma was still alive for me, because I would never forget her. I would always carry in my heart my mother's words, from that little handmade book she had sent me: "Even when you have lost your Mamma, her heart will accompany you forever."

I believe that *La vita, le speranze, la via, l'amore sono il fulcro della esistenza umana!* (Life, hope, the way, and love are the fulcrum of human life!) How was it possible for such a poetic, sensitive young woman to endure the difficult tasks of cruel reality and grueling work, after such an enormous emotional loss? The only strength I relied on was the hope of a better future.

My husband and I moved to Norwalk, so I could be near Adelina. But my husband decided to stay temporarily with his family in Port Chester, to look for a job. Then I got a letter from him announcing that he wanted a divorce. I felt numb. All I could do was keep working.

I had started a new job during the day as a hairdresser. At night, until 1:30 a.m., I worked in a factory in Stamford, making roller skates. I had to dip my hands into a container of grease to put wheels on the roller skates. Little by little, the skin on my hands was destroyed by the harsh grease, and my skin began to peel.

Now that I was separated from my husband, I knew I needed to get a driver's license so that I could be independent. While I was studying for my license, I had to take a taxi from my job in Norwalk to the factory in Stamford. Out of my paycheck of $14.00, I had to pay $13.00. That meant I would have to live off the remaining dollar. I made one dollar a night for two years.

I bought a broken-down old car. I couldn't afford to rent an apartment, so I ended up sleeping in the car night after night. The window was broken, and it was freezing. I had to hide in my car in the parking lot of a shopping center when the trucks came to deliver food early in the morning. I was curled under the seat like a ball of yarn, trying to keep warm. I didn't understand how this could have happened to me. Did I deserve all this pain from this terrible life? I had nowhere to turn. I couldn't call my sister Adelina, who was visiting her husband's family in Italy. I was alone.

I was *pelle e ossa* (skin and bones). Late one night, in desperation, I knocked at the door of a very old lady I knew, asking for a place to sleep. I couldn't stay at her house because of her husband, but she told me to hide in the attic. It was dirty, dusty, and full of mice. I couldn't sleep, but lying on the hard floor was better than shivering all night in the car.

One day, as I was driving, I saw my husband walking along on the sidewalk. I called his name and he turned to look. He couldn't believe that the young woman driving a car was me. I was unrecognizable! We began to spend time together, and eventually we decided to get back together again. We rented an apartment in Harrison, New York. It had no furniture, so we had to sleep on the floor, but to me, it seemed like a soft feather mattress!

Even though I was back with my husband, I still had to endure more grueling jobs. I took a job as an interior decorator during the day. At night I assembled beauty products for the Avon Company. It was very hard for me to stay up until 1:30 a.m. and then go to the next job at 8:00 a.m. in the morning.

During these years, I also worked for upholstery companies. I worked at three different upholstery companies over a period of fifteen years. In addition, I went to private homes to make slipcovers and curtains. My Jewish friends in the business always helped me find work. But these jobs were difficult. They were men's jobs. I had to lift heavy couches and climb ladders holding heavy drapes. I developed a hernia that prevented me from working for nearly a month.

In between my jobs, I had to cook for my husband and take care of the house. I was very organized and could barely rest. I felt it was my duty to set an elegant table and serve a delicious meal. There was no time for a social life or a normal married life. Nothing was normal for me. I'd get up and go to work while it was still dark, and I'd come home after dark. I rarely saw daylight. In the summer, when it was still light at 5:00 p.m., I would arrive home and the landlord would tell me to climb up the fire escape instead of the stairs. I didn't understand why, but I didn't ask. Sometimes I was so exhausted that I fell off the fire escape and hurt myself.

Years passed, and my husband and I were able to save enough money to put a down payment on a new home. We bought a house in Rye Brook, New York. Now we had a large mortgage to keep up. Job after job, day after day, I somehow remained standing tall on my two feet. I was still the best hostess, house-wife and worker. But in the following years, the side effects of my endless overwork left me an empty shell.

CHAPTER ELEVEN

My Health

*A*fter all the years of long hours and strenuous, exhausting jobs, I became really ill. I began to faint at work and had to be admitted to the hospital. Being in the hospital was a relief for me. I didn't have to report to work! Can you imagine that? I opened my eyes and saw the bouquets of flowers on the window sill of my hospital room, and I smiled from happiness, even if I was in pain. Gazing at the flowers lifted my spirits, as it always had since I was a little girl.

When I was released from the hospital, I went back to work, but soon began fainting again. I felt dizzy from weakness. But I forced myself to continue doing the housework: washing the clothes, mending and sewing, cooking beautiful dinners and setting an elegant table.

I was desperate to have a child. When I went to the doctor and was faced with technical medical terminology, I didn't understand what was said to me. I underwent many operations without really comprehending what was being done. It was hard for me to make important life decisions.

When I was first married and working in the sweatshops, I had met Father Rinaldi at church. He was kind and wise, and he became my spiritual advisor and a dear friend as well. After each operation, I would run to Father Rinaldi to confess. I cried about my miserable, unhappy life without a child. Father Rinaldi called me "the noble young lady with a great heart," because I loved children so much. I dreamed constantly of having a child of my own. I would have been such a loving mother if I had had the chance.

I went to church every day. I couldn't carry that cross on my shoulder anymore—the cross of despair, of not being a mother to a sweet, innocent child. I felt so different from other women, like *l'avanzo della morte* (leftover death), as Mamma used to call me. I had tasted death so many times, only to survive for a lifetime of despair. I felt as if I were in a desert without a drop of water to refresh my lips with the desire to live.

Even now, when I am sad, when melancholy chokes my throat, that marvelous miracle—the smile of a child—restores me and gives me vitality, joy and lively hope. My heart smiles too. My heart never ages and still desires its rights of happiness, vitality, love and peace that only a child can give as a precious gift.

My journey from one doctor to the other, from New York to Connecticut, never ended. Each doctor promised me that with the "right" operation, I would be able to fulfill my dream of motherhood. The time went by and nothing happened.

I finally decided to turn to adoption as the last option. But at that time, my husband and I were too poor to qualify to adopt a child. I didn't even know if my husband would welcome an adopted child. My father-in-law berated me, calling me *albero secco* (dry tree), and saying, "We don't want a bastard in this house!"

But I refused to give up. I decided to fly to Italy to adopt a baby. I would have crossed the mountains in bare feet to hold a baby in my arms, to have a child whose heart would beat with love just for me. My first stop was at the orphanage in Penne, a city close to Loreto Aprutino. How strange it is how life cycles around! Here I was, twenty years later, at the foundling hospital where many of the poor women who had been raped during the war had brought their unwanted babies to be adopted. I walked through the orphanage with the nun. A little blonde girl with curly hair and blue eyes ran smiling to me.

The nun said, "That's your daughter!" But the next day, the nun called me and said that the little girl's mother had decided not to give her up.

Once again, I was denied the adoption because we didn't have enough money. My husband couldn't fly to Italy to help me because he had to work in New York. I couldn't continue the search in Italy any longer. I had to go back to New York to report to work. My heart was shattered. But my husband didn't even seem to care. He was a man from another planet.

I had no choice but to return to New York and go back to work. To add to my misery, my father-in-law taunted me cruelly. Over and over, he called me *albero secco*. "You can't bear children and we don't want a bastard in this house!" he would repeat. My husband, too weak-willed to take my side, was silent. I was numb with pain. Those terrible, insulting words hammered in my head and threatened to kill my soul.

My desire to have a baby never died. I never gave up. I went under the doctor's knife at least seven times, but the results were always the same: no child. Then one day, after all those years and all those operations, I found out that it was my husband who couldn't have a child.

The secret came out! However, it was too late.

After all the intrusive operations, I was deprived forever of what belonged to me: my right of motherhood and womanhood. What a shock for me! My heart was forever broken, collapsing like a sand castle blown by the wind into a million grains of sand.

I still cry, even now, remembering the pain of not being a mother. I always looked at children walking by. I wanted to see their smiles and touch their skin, soft as roses. My mind and my soul were forever destroyed and could never be mended. I asked myself again and again how this could have happened to me, and how I could consider myself human after all this pain. I had no love, no tenderness. I felt lifeless.

My health continued to deteriorate, but I never withdrew from my responsibilities to work and take care of the house. I never went out for meals. I always cooked and entertained at my home, trying to create a family atmosphere to the best of my abilities. I cooked wonderful dinners, making all the foods from scratch. The aroma of my delicious dishes emanated from my kitchen and wafted through the neighborhood. Sometimes I invited my neighbors, or the kids on the street, to fill up my table so that I felt I had a family.

I was married, but I was alone. The hope in my heart was still alive and would carry me into tomorrow. Maybe my life could still change. I lived without a tender kiss or embrace, without making love, without everything that a woman needs to fulfill her emotional and physical life. There was nothing left of my marriage. We lived like ghosts. We became scared of each other. If we met on the stairs, my husband would flatten himself against the opposite railing so that he wouldn't touch me, even by mistake. After nearly twenty-five years, my husband and I separated for good.

CHAPTER TWELVE

The Separation

After my husband and I separated, I had to work even harder. Now I had on my shoulders the full responsibility of paying the mortgage to keep my home in Rye Brook. When anything went wrong in the house, I didn't know what to do. The boiler burst. The radiators banged and clattered. I was afraid to open the door after dark. One night a man knocked, but I was too frightened to answer. He called through the door, "I'm your neighbor. Your house is on fire!" He came in to help me, and we called the fire department. It turned out that I hadn't known to fill the furnace with water!

I was alone, but I was blessed with an old friendship that had been kindled before I got married. My friend's name was Lucy, but I called her "Mamma Lucy." She was there for me in times of trouble, sharing my tears and my pain. She was ready to help me, without fail, and she became my best friend.

Every night, I cooked for myself, but I always called Lucy to join me for dinner. Those dinners were crying times: bitter tears of a lonely young, abused woman. Lucy said, "I will do anything for you, Giovanna. Don't cry anymore. I am sorry that things didn't go well for you, but I know God will work things out for you one day. I pray every day for that day to come. Don't cry, please. Don't cry!" I responded, "I am okay, Lucy. I am okay." I tried to be strong, but the pain in my heart got the best of me.

Lucy often said that I would make a great businesswoman, and she was right in the end. She told me, "You are so talented, lovely, and elegant. You'll see, your personality will help you, and one day you will have the happiness you deserve."

I started interviewing for jobs in the fur business in Stamford, Connecticut. I was offered a job, but before starting, I was told that I had to take a lie detector test. That was a terrifying experience. In a dark room, with policemen surrounding me, I was interrogated like a thief! I felt as though I were strapped to the electric chair in the dark, with those machines recording my responses to the questions. I still remember the trauma and fear I felt. I passed the test, but the fear of the struggle never left me.

I worked in the fur business in Stamford for some time, but I eventually lost the job because of my looks and elegance, and the envy of another woman whom I had helped. She told me outright, "I am envious of your elegance and the way you look." When she told me that, I dropped the sharp fur knife I was holding, and it stuck into my leg. I was wearing a white linen suit, but I had to keep working until I could go upstairs to the kitchen to get some water to clean off the blood.

This was a women I had helped. She had begged me to bring her along to the job. I brought her to my house to teach her to sew, before taking her to the company. She seemed so grateful. But as soon as she walked into the company, and saw how respected I was for my elegance and design skills, she became envious.

After that, something changed at work. The way she manipulated other people caused them to become cold to me. I pleaded with the manager, "Please fire me so I can qualify for unemployment." He said, "I can't do that. There's work here for you and you are a good designer. You never should have brought her here." I had to quit the job.

Once again, I was alone and searching for work. Without a job, I came down with pneumonia.

In my life, there were many Jewish people, with whom I found comfort and friendship. They helped me in every sense, and gave me the knowledge and strength to survive and to find work. I soon found another job in a tailor shop in Mt. Kisco. While working in Mt. Kisco, I had an accident. I fell from a staircase and broke my tailbone. Somehow, I managed to deal with the pain, and I kept working endlessly, as always. Every day, my eyes were swollen from tears. I could barely see. But I was so afraid of losing my job that I wouldn't stop working, even for half an hour. I worked without eating. I worked in physical pain.

Every day, after work, I went directly to the hospital to be treated for the pain. I lay on a hospital bed with an intravenous drip until 4:00 a.m., when I would ask the nurse to take out the needles so that I could get back to work on time.

One night, on my way home from Mt. Kisco, my car's transmission died. I found myself stranded in the middle of Highway 287 East, going back home to Rye Brook. It was pouring rain and I had no coat or umbrella. At midnight, in the cold and dark, with no cell phone, I stood shivering on the side of the highway, afraid to be run over by the cars racing by. I was completely wet and as frozen as an icicle.

I couldn't stop shivering. I stood and waited for hours, but still no one would stop. I finally saw in the distance a pair of lights that looked like a faraway animal's eyes. They were the high beams of a car. Finally, someone was kind enough to pull over to see what was wrong. A gentleman stopped and helped me. I finally arrived home at 2:00 a.m., wet, chilled, and distraught.

Those hours spent outside in the nasty weather took their toll on my health. My pneumonia got worse. I was sick for weeks, barely able to get food and unable to go to work. Pale, weak and thin as a stick, I could hardly stand up. I got sicker and sicker. I lost my job again. Every afternoon, I would hold my head in my hands. My head felt like a stone. My worries and fears grew bigger and bigger until I felt as though my head was exploding.

I went without work for months and months. Finally, thanks to some Jewish friends who helped me again in this moment of need, I found a job working for a Temple. I did anything. I made beautiful covers for Torahs for the Synagogue, doing needlepoint, cutting and fixing slip covers. I even did interior decorating on yachts for the Norwalk Marina in Norwalk.

When I was making covers for the Torahs, the Rabbi reminded me not to drop them because they were sacred. However, I accidentally dropped them several times because they were too heavy for such a small woman as I was. I had to turn them under sewing machine, and sometimes they did fall. Afraid to be scolded, I never told the Rabbi!

After this, again I went for eighteen months with no job and no prospects. I knocked relentlessly at every door. Finally, thanks to a close friend, I went to Manhattan for an interview at a fur company. After that interview, I was offered a position in their New Jersey location, making fur coats. I was very nervous about driving to New Jersey.

For years, my alarm clock went off routinely every morning at 4:00 a.m., but every night I lay anxiously in bed with my eyes wide open. I had sleepless nights for many years. I was always terrified of getting lost on the way to work, especially because I was so tired all the time.

My first day of work at the fur company in New Jersey was not pleasant. At this company, the employees were mostly men, and I felt like an outsider. There I met two male designers who made my work impossible and my life miserable. On that first day, I was left all by myself without any help or orientation. I was asked to perform impossible tasks.

I could only stand this unfair workplace for three never-ending days. Abused again, as in the past, and denied financial rewards, I found the courage to quit. While driving back home at a very late hour, over the Tappan Zee Bridge, I felt as though the heavy bridge was on top of my head, weighing me down to the ground. I said to myself, "This is a real curse!" Enough was enough! But my misfortune was going to continue, and the worst had yet to come.

I closed my eyes and tried like a delicate butterfly to shake off the dust from my fragile wings and to spread my colorful wings to fly. I tried to take off, flying towards the sky where for a moment of pure joy, I saw the face of my dear mother, Lucia, smiling at me. My mother seemed to whisper in my ear, "You, my beautiful little butterfly, keep spreading your delicate and precious wings. Don't give up. You are strong. Mamma will always be with you!"

My eyes were wet with painful tears and I reopened them to find myself lying in my bed. I felt as if I had been touched by an angel, and my heart, that had been broken into pieces, felt magically mended after the appearance of my spiritual guide: my loving mother, Lucia.

CHAPTER THIRTEEN

The Fur Business

Four months after I had the vision of my mother, one of my furrier acquaintances told me that there was an elegant fur designing business for sale in Bronxville, New York. I went to the boutique and talked to the owner. She said, "You are elegant and clever. You will make a good business owner." I only had twenty-four hours to decide. The owner's husband called me and said, "My wife says you will make a great businesswoman. She's crazy about you. Please buy the business!" He was very ill, and died soon after.

I bought the business and found a friend to partner with me. This was the beginning of a new chapter in my life. It was a chance of a lifetime. My wish, so long repressed, to express my talents of creativity and artistry were about to come true. I would finally have the opportunity to create my own business designing furs, and to freely be myself.

The boutique was elegant and beautiful, and my partner and I began to reach out to the existing clientele. We cordially invited each of the customers to visit the shop, where we made them feel at home, learned about their lives, and built a relationship. The many sophisticated ladies of Bronxville and the surrounding towns were loyal patrons.

The business flourished better than ever, but my partner and I began to have difficulties. Plenty of elegant customers were coming to the shop, and sending their friends too. But greed had become an issue, and the partnership began to dissolve. One day, as I was sitting in a coffee shop, a policeman came over and slapped a paper in my hand. I was being served! My partner wanted to buy me out for a certain sum of money. I cried, "Oh God! Again?"

I had to find a lawyer, so I talked with several different attorneys. I made a counter-offer to buy out my partner. I found a smart and lovely lawyer with whom I had a great rapport, and we began to work together. Then she went on vacation to Mexico and was run over by a train and killed. She was running to catch the train and slipped. What a beautiful life, cut short! This tragedy touched me very deeply. And I was alone again, hoping for a solution to my problem.

In the middle of this crisis, I had to rush back to

Italy to attend to my dear brother, Antonio, who was ill with cancer. When I saw him, I barely recognized him. My big, handsome brother, who used to protect me when we were children, was so wasted away that his fragile body weighed just sixty-five pounds. I sat for hours by his side, cradling his head on my shoulder as he lay dying. I had to ask someone to lift his head off me because it was so heavy. I went to the kitchen for a glass of water, and suddenly felt pneumonia coming on. I went back to the house to try to rest, but it was impossible. My pneumonia worsened. During the night, I developed a high fever and started vomiting. I tried to call to my sister, who was snoring in the other room. "Maria, help, please, help me. I am dying!" She didn't hear me. The night passed fitfully, as I lay burning with fever. At 4:00 a.m. the phone rang. I was barely able to get up to answer it, and I slipped in my own vomit as I grabbed the receiver. When I finally picked up the phone, Piera, my niece, was on the other end of the line. She told me that Antonio was dead. She asked me, "Aunt, how do you feel? We are going to come to you right away. We love you!" She had arranged for a pulmonary specialist to come to the house in the morning, with Piera's husband, who was also a doctor. When the specialist saw how ill I was, he told me that I couldn't leave the country until I had fully recovered.

My sister Adelina went back to New York to her family. I remained in Italy, where my family cared for me and cooked for me until I was healthy again. I slowly began to feel better. When I was finally able to go back to America, everything had changed at my business. The conflict with my business partner had increased. We didn't talk to each other, even when we were working side by side in the boutique. The nastiness became unbearable and I decided to buy out my partner with a lump sum of money.

I was by myself once again, about to face yet another challenge. After building a successful business in Bronxville, with loyal and respectful clients who loved my designs and artistry, vandals began to destroy all that I had built with sacrifice, devotion, and honesty.

Every night I was awakened by the phone ringing. It was the police telling me to run to my boutique. All over the window of my shop were signs written in red ink, saying, "Don't kill the animals!" My window, so elegantly decorated, was covered by a big sign glued to the glass, and blood-red paint splashed on the windowpanes. On the weekends, my neighbor, who owned a liquor store near my shop, would call to tell me that my beautiful shop window was vandalized again with signs from the animal rights group.

At the height of the season, in November, when it was time for my customers to pick up their stored fur coats, I wasn't able to open the shop door. The vandals had poured crazy glue into the keyhole and I was locked outside my own shop, with no way to get in. I could hear the phone ringing inside the shop. Customers started to arrive, only to find me standing outside my shop, angry and frustrated. I had to call the locksmith to come change the lock and save the situation.

It was painful for me to see such devastation. My loyal clients would bring me flowers to cheer me up. Every day I went to the shop and tried to smile, but business was slowing down. When customers saw the damage to my windows, they passed by and didn't come in.

I spent long hours in my shop, afraid to leave. I had to think. I had to figure this out! I had to try to serve my devoted clients faithfully. But almost every night, I received a phone call from the police, telling me that someone was trying to break in to try to steal the fur coats. Again, in the middle of the night, I had to travel to Bronxville to see the damage done to my shop window.

I couldn't rest. I loved my business so much that I couldn't bear the idea of losing it. The fear tormented me because I was all by myself. My business was my baby.

I decided to install video cameras in and around my shop, with the hope of videotaping the people who were the cause of this vandalism. The next time the vandal came, the video cameras caught images of a man with a long ponytail. But it wasn't enough for the police to arrest him. The police said to me, "So many men have a ponytail! How do we know which one it is?"

Finally, one morning at 4:00 a.m., an old man who was out walking witnessed the man with the ponytail in the act of writing on my window. With liquid acid, he wrote the word VANITY. That strong acid destroyed the glass, and my window collapsed. The old man wrote down the license plate number of the perpetrator's car, and gave it to another merchant, who told me about it later on. The old man didn't want to give his name, but he told the merchant, "I see that the nice lady's business next door is being destroyed!"

I went to the police again. This time the police worked very fast, and finally the man was caught. At the police station, he confessed that he had committed the crime. When the police asked me if I wanted to press charges against him, I told them to let him go. However, because I was afraid of being attacked, I did request a restraining order against him. The

Bronxville police ordered him not to come within several miles of my shop. A few months later, the perpetrator committed suicide, throwing himself under a New York City subway train. The police called me to tell me not to be afraid anymore!

The Christmas season arrived and all my loyal clients from Bronxville helped me to decorate my newly replaced windows. That year, I won the prize from the Chamber of Commerce for the most beautiful decorations.

In the spring, I was asked by the Bronxville Women's Club to present a fashion show, which was a great honor. I got busy organizing the models and the flowers and table decorations. Most of the models were my customers. The police escorted me with the furs to the Women's Club. A Broadway singer and actress who lived in Bronxville was the announcer for the show. She provided the commentary, describing each coat and design by name, "And now, here is Jacqueline, wearing a magnificent Russian sable." At the end of the show, wearing a beautiful suit with a cameo, I walked the runway with my model. I was extremely grateful to my distinguished clients for giving me the gift of confidence to be myself, and to walk with pride. My elegant, classy fashion shows were a great success. To this day, I am still appreciative of the Women's

Club for their support and encouragement.

About a week after the fashion show in Bronx-ville, I was invited by the Scarsdale Women's Club to take part their fashion show. I showed my own unique fur designs, and again my elegant customers were my models.

For once in my life, I felt ten feet tall from the pride of owning my own business. I felt as if I owned the world. What an accomplishment, after all that suffering! What gratifying freedom to be able to work for myself and to gain higher status. I felt at the same level as my distinguished and sophisticated customers.

Bronxville reminded me of the lovely town of Pescara, near Loreto Aprutino. One night, before I had even dreamed of owning my own business, I had driven through Bronxville and seen all the beautiful little boutiques. I thought to myself then, "Wouldn't it be wonderful to have my own shop here?" Two years later, I did!

When young people came into the shop, they'd ask my advice about what to buy. "Giovanna, what should I get for my sister?" I'd answer, "Why not matching fur gloves and a headband?" Then the other sister would call and ask the same question. I'd offer the same advice. When they opened the pack-ages, they had a wonderful surprise! I loved to play little games with my customers.

One of my specialties was to refashion fur coats for customers. I'd refashion an old coat and update the style, often adding new skin and fur.

When it was time to shop for furs and materials, I had to go to the fashion district in New York City. I didn't know the city streets well. Every two weeks, I'd drive into the city, park my car and get lost walking around Manhattan.

The furrier's showroom was on the 22nd floor. When I arrived, I had to wait while they opened the gates before I could enter. I'd bring with me a list of what I wanted to buy. An employee would bring down racks of furs to show me. I'd examine them, make my choice, and then I had to make an offer.

When I was refashioning coats, I had to cut the skins to perfectly match the already existing coat. This was a very difficult task that took a lot of concentration. I'd be so nervous that sometimes I'd asked people to sit with me! I'd take the measurements and then cut the pelts, with the skin side facing up and the fur facing down. Then I had to tack the skin to the table to stretch it to exactly the correct measurements. When the refashioned coat was ready, I called the customer to come into the shop for a fitting.

Working with fur and fur patterns is completely

different from fabric and clothing patterns. My sisters, Gabriella and Maria, were *modeliste* (fashion designers) and every season, they supplied me with brand-new patterns that they had created in Italy. The talent and art of designing runs in my family. When I designed furs and clothing, I felt proud of the Acciavatta family and our heritage of fashion design.

As a fur designer, I was invited to the fashion shows of Valentino, Ralph Lauren, Armani, and other famous designers. But in my shop, I was down to earth. At night I swept the floor and put out the garbage. In the morning, when I arrived at the shop, faxes—all addressed to "Sir"—waited for me on the floor. At that time there were no female fur designers! At Christmas, customers would call from the city and ask, "Did my wife see anything she liked? Would you pack it up for her?" I loved wrapping the beautiful furs in delicate tissue paper and creating a fancy gift for my clients. Now the beauty of life flourished all around me.

One sunny day, a beautiful young woman by the name of Lisa, and her mother, Giuseppina, were looking in the window of my shop. The mother and daughter were both beautiful. They walked in to admire a coat, and we began to chat together. The young woman, already a lawyer, was as lovely as the sun. I asked her if she'd like to work for me and she accepted. She agreed to work on the weekends, when I needed extra help. Every morning I would see her walking by with her hair blowing in the breeze. When Lisa sat in the shop, looking like a star with her long hair flowing down on one side, customers thought she was my daughter! We made a connection right away, and could talk for hours. We became as close as a mother and daughter, and continue to respect and love each other and our families. The customers loved Lisa and came back again and again to the shop. Even now, our friendship is unique, and always will be.

I also enjoyed having my nieces assist me in the store. One Saturday, my nieces, Virginia and Lucia, were helping me in the shop. Virginia, who was blonde and sophisticated, had green eyes like mine. Lucia, who had the same name as my Mamma, was brunette and petite like her Aunt Giovanna. They were always looking in the mirror and admiring themselves. They were as vain as I was! Virginia would try on every coat in the showroom and twirl around in front of the mirror. My two sisters, Maria and Gabriella, both successful designers in Italy, came to my shop every year to design *la moda Italiana* (Italian fashion), for my customers. Little by little, life was all mine. I was finally receiving the gift that I deserved. Now, as I tried to climb that wall, slick with oil, I was able to grab onto something that was mine.

During the time that my business was flourishing, I often went out with my friends to piano bars to dance. Many young men asked me to dance cheek to cheek, and I enjoyed the distinction of mixing with business people. One evening a young businessman, very elegant, asked me to dance. He was in the the computer business, and was about to leave for a business trip. He liked me very much and said he would call me from California. He did call, and told me he'd be coming back in two weeks. I liked him too and my hopes began to rise. But he was killed in an accident on the way to the airport. Once again, tragedy intruded on my life.

When Maria and Gabriella visited, they stayed with me in my house in Rye Brook. We ate and talked together, just as we had when we were in the bosom of our family long before. With colored threads, we were reweaving our safe family nest all around us. All day long at her house in Norwalk, my oldest sister, Adelina, cooked and baked cakes. She made elegant meals for us and set the table with embroidered cloths and crystal glasses. A centerpiece of fresh flowers always stood in the middle of the table. She would wait for us, her three sisters, to come from Bronxville to have dinner. Other members of the family came too: Adelina's other two children, Antonio and Vinny, with their children, and the family of my brother-in-law Vinny (Adelina's husband), and always some neighbors too. We became a close Italian-American family, and my sister's table was always filled with laughter and the love of family and friends.

After all the physical and mental abuse, begging for jobs, working at the most demeaning jobs that nearly killed me, I could finally say that I was free! How sad and lonely my life had been before. But now, thanks to my ability to create and develop my own business, I was happy. I felt the thrill of my customers' support and enthusiasm for my unique creations. I said to myself, "I own this place. This is my place." For me it was like a dream.

I was even offered the opportunity to do a commercial on television. While planting flowers in my garden (I loved to garden like my mother Lucia), I saw some men with TV video cameras approaching my home. They were from Channel 12, our local news channel. They asked me if I wanted to make a commercial. There I was, in my gardening clothes! I rushed inside to find something pretty to wear. Even though I was very self-conscious and a perfectionist, I decided to do the commercial anyway. I was so happy and grateful for the opportunity to be recognized and appreciated for all my devoted work.

However, once again, this dreamy life wasn't going to last too long. *Nella mia vita non ho trovato mai pace!* (In my life I have never found peace!) My life is and will always be at the end of my days, a life of despair, of pain, of endless tears. The only comfort is the hope of a better future.

My country is the colorful cane

In my years of absence, I was dreaming of reliving with joy those happy moments
with the luminous sun, to warm my heart in that beloved garden in blossom.

While I look around to find my place in the world of wonders,
my heart is divided in two, cut by a double-sided blade.

I look again for the support of that colorful cane to give life to my life
with harmony, a gesture, a word with love notes under the starry night with the perfume of dew.

But my dream was so short. A little lantern with the weak light of a dying heart.

That little light, that little hope between the oceans and those mountains was nothing.

Not to fall suddenly, slowly I lean on that colorful little cane.

As soon as I touch it with a finger, it collapses to the ground. It's only fine paper made of infinite colors.

Those colors browse my mind page by page, like an old calendar.

My mind closes on those painful memories of my dreams.

Italy Calls Me

I was over the moon because my fur business was flourishing like a sailboat flying fast on the waters of the ocean of success, towards the horizon in the distance. I loved my elegant clients in Bronxville. They were my life and it was an honor and privilege for me to serve them with passion and dedication. They loved me and respected me as their fashion designer.

But my heart was thirsty for love, and every day I missed my family back in Italy. I was homesick. My family missed me too, and constantly invited me to come back. I started to dream of the life I had left behind.

In my mind, I tasted the flavor of the sparkling fresh air of my country. I dreamed of sitting on a bench with my schoolmates, telling them about my life during all the years of my absence. I rode with my sisters on the bus along the Adriatic coast, with all the windows down and my hair caressed by the warm gentle wind. I liked to ride in the front of the bus, close to the conductor, so that I could catch the views of nature: the giant green palm trees against the blue sky, and the colorful flowers that decorated the streets along the beach. All those waterfalls and fountains of colors and lights!

I thought of the days when my family and I could travel on the train for free, going anywhere we liked because my father worked for the railroad. I longed to live those days again, tasting every single moment of childhood experienced in my youth. I remembered the exquisite drinks, the salty taste of fresh fish, just caught and so delicious that my mouth watered just thinking about it. I wanted to restore my body and mind. I wanted to embrace my family, who had been there for me all my life.

I dreamed of going back in time. I was walking along the beach, so elegant with its colorful umbrellas, beach chairs, and the little *casotti* (bathing huts) whose colors shone brilliantly in the sunlight. In the distance, the umbrellas looked like rainbows, reflecting the emerald-green sea in the golden tones of the sunset. In my hand I held an ice cream cone, licking it slowly and savoring the delicious ice cream that dripped and melted the crisp, buttery cone. The warm wind caressed my face like a young girl. I listened to the orchestra under the starry sky while the ocean waves tickled my feet, planted in the warm sand. I was comforted and caressed by the waves.

All this seemed so real in my mind that I decided to move back to Italy. I was already wishing for it, but one more time I was denied hope, love, and the joy of life. This was my dream, but again my dream was going to break, like a crystal glass, into million pieces.

I began packing my belongings in preparation for the move back to Italy, but I was also aware of a painful feeling. Perhaps it was because the wings of that young butterfly girl had already lost their colors from the bitter tears she had spilled. How could I cross the ocean again, carrying such an overwhelming burden, so heavy for my tiny, overworked wings?

I had to let go of my sweet little shop—my home away from home—that I had paid for with so many sacrifices. My design boutique, so elegant and warm, that I loved with all my heart! I felt sick inside. I knew I also had to let go of my chic friends who respected me as one of the kindest and most elegant women in Bronxville. I found the courage to collect my most precious things: brand-name clothing and expensive purses, dresses and accessories, all chosen with the style and finesse that had characterized me since I was a little girl.

The time arrived to sell my house and my

business. I donated most of my belongings to charity. When I saw my house looking so empty and naked, I felt naked too. I started doubting myself. I didn't know if I truly wanted to go back to Italy. I felt a sixth sense and started calling to my Mamma, asking for her protection. But this time, I felt that my mother, even in Paradise, had lost her power to help me, her fragile Giovannina.

As my departure for Italy came closer and closer, my fear was becoming a reality. I cried painful tears as I thought about saying goodbye to all that I had built during forty-five years of struggle, pain, sickness, humiliation, abuse, loneliness, and most of all, the absence of love.

I remember one last moment before leaving my home. I was in my kitchen, leaning towards the door of my refrigerator with my head down, thinking, "What are you doing, Giovanna? Are you about to jump in the lake?"

I was also leaving my sister Adelina and my four nieces whom I loved very much. It was bittersweet, because I knew that Adelina was rich in so many ways, and happy in America. I was sure she wouldn't miss me as much as I was going to miss her. I agonized about this, because I loved my sister so deeply.

While I was preparing my papers and

documents, my family was anxiously getting ready to welcome me back to Italy. They asked me what I wanted when I arrived. I was longing to taste those delicious homemade tortellini and sweets that I remembered from my childhood. I knew that when I landed at the airport in Rome, I would once again taste these childhood delicacies.

After the long hours of flying, I was disoriented and very anxious. When we arrived at dawn, my family was first in line, waiting for me. My sister Maria kissed me, and that embrace lasted an instant for me. My family was hugging me and filling my mouth with sweets and *bocconcini* (small mozzarella balls), freshly made for me.

But more trouble was ahead. *Non c'è pace tra gli ulivi.* There was no peace under the olive trees for me. I didn't make it past the gate. Two Italian *gendarmi* shoved their badges in my face. I cried, "Oh my God! What on earth have I done?" My mind was racing as fast as a supersonic jet, trying to understand what was happening. One of the gendarmi said to follow them with my luggage. Trembling with fear, I felt my body covered in a cold sweat. In a small, windowless room, I was asked to remove my documents from my bags. I was carrying some cash and my most precious jewelry, that I had bought with the sweat of my hard work.

They examined my bankbook, where the sales of my house and business were recorded. The worst came. They interrogated me. "Where did you get this money?" They kept asking the same question, "Who gave you this money to come back to Italy? Where did you get this money?" The gendarmi yelled in my face, "Be quiet! Leave here, if you don't want problems!"

My sister Maria was waiting anxiously for me. My other sister, Gabriella, was calling my cell phone nonstop to find out what it was happening.

Then the tax officers stopped me to question me. Once again, I was sweating cold and hot from fear, and shaking uncontrollably. I developed a fever so high that the gendarmi let me go. Maria picked me up and we took the car back to Gabriella's house in Montesilvano, in the province of Pescara.

Gabriella was waiting on the balcony to see the car arriving in the distance. Her little sister, Giovanna, was coming back home and she couldn't contain her joy! The table at her home was set for a queen, with a beautiful handmade white lace tablecloth, china dishes, tall crystal glasses and freshly cut red, pink, and purple roses from my mother's garden.

When I entered Gabriella's dining room, I felt spoiled and pampered like a little girl. I was treated to a delicious lunch filled with the flavors of our family's food and a pinch of love in every dish. I was given all the attention in the world, with everyone going out of their way to seat me comfortably with soft pillows, and most of all with love.

But I also felt like a foreigner in my own country. I was having a serious problem with the Italian law enforcement, who treated me like a Martian who had just stepped off her own planet. I had hoped to find some well-deserved peace and tranquillity under the Italian sky, but this beautiful dream was not for me. I couldn't live as I had in my childhood memories.

I said, *"Fermate il mondo, voglio scendere! Vado per trovare grazia e ho trovato ingiustizia!"* (Stop the world, I want to get down! I look for kindness and I find injustice!)

A few days later, I hadn't even had time to pick up my luggage before the gendarmi ordered me to go to the *Questura* (police department) every morning, to stand in line with the immigrants! The Questura kept asking me to provide many different documents to prove I was an Italian citizen. But I was born in Loreto Aprutino and was raised in Capelle and Montesilvano, Italy! Was this a joke? Why should there be so much pain and suffering again for me?

After many months of the same tedious

morning routine, I was given the same rude attitude from one of the state employees, who kept trying to find something wrong with my papers. I was becoming more and more puzzled and mentally drained. I started doubting my identity. I asked myself, "Who am I? Where do I belong?" I was told by the Questura that every time I left my home in Montesilvano, I had to report to the police. They made me feel like a criminal or a terrorist.

While I was struggling to understand what was happening to me and trying to make the best of it, family conflicts blossomed. My family was not supportive of my frustration and anger. They took it personally and started asking me, "What's the matter? You don't like Italy anymore? Your country? Your family? We've done so much for you. What's wrong? Why aren't you happy here? What can we do? We love you!"

Things were getting worse each day. I tried to find peace by looking for my own place to live. But my sisters started fighting about where I should live and how close to whom. I made my own decision and bought an elegant apartment on the beach, quite far from everyone. But I felt lost. No matter where I went, I couldn't find peace.

Without a car, I was still dependent on my family for my everyday needs. My sisters were still kind and cooked for me and with me. But even though they tried to make me feel at home, I still felt strange in my own country and lonely inside myself. I started to get sick again. My lungs collapsed and I went to the hospital several times.

After many months, my luggage from America finally arrived on the shores of the Adriatic. My new apartment looked elegant and charming with its new furniture. However, it was very humid, and the humidity of the place caused pains in my legs. I felt as if my legs were being sucked into the tiled floor. I developed pain in my hip bones, and eventually I needed a hip replacement. But I didn't have the surgery right away.

My dear, sensitive sister Gabriella was so close to me that she felt every pain and sorrow with me. As a result of depression and stress, she slipped into a profound coma. While I was in and out of the hospital every fifteen days, I was shocked and destroyed by the news of my sister's coma. There was a terrible heat wave during that summer in Italy, and both the pain and the heat were unbearable.

Even if I was in pain, I found that inner strength I was born with, to comfort my big sister. For months, I sat every night and day in front of the little window inside the hospital, watching my sister lying in a coma. It was awful to see that beautiful woman with her shiny chestnut hair, plump ruby lips, and brown eyes, lying lifeless with all those tubes around her in the cold hospital bed.

One day, my sister Gabriella's hand began to move! The doctor communicated the great news to my family. When I arrived, running to her bedside, the first thing she said to me was, "Giovanna, I just listened to the Mass. Today is the Feast of the Immaculate Conception. It is December 8th!" I didn't know that myself. I was breathless! How could she know that? Gabriella told me that she had died. She had had a near-death experience, and had seen other dead people.

My hip pain continued to worsen and I decided that I needed to go back to New York, not only for my operation, but for good. The cost of an operation in a big city like Bologna, which had the best doctors, would have meant leaning on my family. I didn't want to be a weight on them. I was too independent to allow that, and even if I didn't have the money, I would never ask for help. My heart was broken again.

When she heard that I had decided to return to America, Gabriella's health took a turn for the worse. She slipped into a terrible depression and remained lying down in her bed, ready to die.

Spring arrived. Everything was in blossom. All

the streets were perfumed by the sweet smell of the pink, white, and red oleanders and the beautiful red climbing *campanule* (bellflowers) of Montesilvano. In the distance, the ocean sparkled with the silver reflections of a warm sunny day. But inside, I felt dark as midnight. I was leaving again, lost in the world, with nowhere to go, no hopes, and no dreams— nothing but sorrow and crying.

Then it was Easter, and time for the family to sit together around a magnificently decked-out table, piled with all the traditional dishes of the season. But I felt as if it were the Last Supper. In the previous weeks, Gabriella had become sicker and sicker, and had begun to vomit blood. On Easter Sunday, she somehow found the strength to get up, even if in her heart she knew that this was going to be her last supper with our family.

On that morning, before we went to Maria's house for the big meal, Gabriella came into my room and gave me an enormous chocolate Easter egg with a beautiful blue silk bow. She said in a grim voice, "Here is a wallet with some money for everything you need when you arrive in New York. Have a safe trip and be well. I love you!"

When Gabriella entered the dining room at Maria's house, she walked like an austere queen in her exquisite sky-blue silk dress. Her long shiny hair blinded our eyes and her red lips contrasted strangely with her pale white face. Her smile shone all around the room, as if the the sun's rays were lighting it from within, but her eyes were lost in a lifeless stare.

I held onto that angelic vision of my beloved sister, but not for long.

Right after dinner, Gabriella went to the bathroom and began vomiting blood. She never liked to complain. When it was over, she walked as if nothing had happened towards the balcony, looking into the emptiness under the blue sky. She asked Maria to call her son-in-law, Alfredo. When he arrived, Gabriella suffocated to death in front of all the family, in the worst way imaginable. She was transformed into an unrecognizable image of death.

That night the whole family stood around her cold, dead body, reciting the rosary. Maria didn't want me to leave Italy, and she offered to help me to stay, but I didn't want to listen. Something was telling me to leave, even if I was devastated.

The funeral was the next morning. Fifteen days later, I flew again with my weak wings, my broken heart, and my crushed soul back to nothing, back to emptiness. At the airport in Rome, ready to fly to New York, I stood with only my cane, my sorrow, and my eyes full of tears under the Italian sky that was bearing down on my head like a marble boulder. That heavy sky squashed me down to the ground.

I was still without a country and without a home. In my years of absence from Italy, I had been dreaming of reliving those happy moments in the luminous sun, warming my heart in that beloved garden of blossoming flowers. While I looked around to find my place in the world of wonders, my heart was divided in two, cut by a sharp blade.

I was a stranger in Paradise. All I could do was lean on my cane, but that cane was just thin paper that couldn't sustain my body. As soon as I touched it with my fingers, it collapsed all the way down to the ground, because it was only made of little shreds of paper. My memory is like an old calendar with closed pages and a glimmer of light between the oceans and mountains of my country. Only a weak ray of dying light from a lantern is left of those times when I had hopes of living in harmony, dancing with my love under the stars, with that perfumed dew from the roses in my mother's garden.

Such a short dream. My dream flew away, leaving me with an eternal pain in my heart. My dream flew away like autumn leaves carried by a cold wind, together with the hopes and dreams of a young girl, never to be fulfilled.

CHAPTER FIFTEEN

New York is My Home

Adelina, my oldest sister, was waiting for my return to America. She invited all her friends and family to host a wonderful dinner to celebrate my return to New York. As soon as I opened the door, the tantalizing aromas from the kitchen and the magic of childhood memories inebriated my senses. My sister tried to do her best to welcome me back.

But my heart was empty and there was nothing that could have been done or said to make me feel better. Lost in the world, this was worse than before. I had lost my sister Gabriella. I had lost my country, and I was becoming sicker and sicker. I felt that I had no voice, no hopes, no future anymore. I only had the devastating memory that ripped my heart and mind apart from my dear sister Gabriella, dead forever, underground in the cold cemetery of Montesilvano.

My sister Adelina cooked as if for a queen.

She was able to cook the most exquisite meats and pastas, and forty different kinds of sweets. Adelina's artistry was also displayed by the table setting. The embroidered napkins were presented like a deck of cards. The linen tablecloth had been handmade by our mother. The glasses were lead crystal; the base of each glass was covered by lace embroidery, and the china dishes were decorated in unique designs.

A tall crystal vase sat at the center of the table, full of fresh flowers just cut from the garden in Adelina's back yard. Her flower arrangements looked so professional! Adelina had an infinite love for flowers and each time she went shopping, she would come back with armloads of them to make her house feel more homey.

My nieces and nephews stood in their elegant clothes at the dining room table, welcoming me. *"Zia Giovanna! Zia Giovanna!"* But Zia Giovanna was dead inside.

What was I going to do?

My life was painful again, and my hip pain was increasing. I had no medical insurance. I went to Norwalk to consult with the doctors about my hip pain. The doctor said, "Madam, you will need a major operation on your hip."

That awful news turned me into a different person. I was without a country again, and I was without insurance. Restlessly, I went from one doctor to another. The cortisone shots I was given to ease the pain were not effective enough, and they were slowly destroying my body. I made the final decision not to go back to Italy, even facing all these obstacles. I called my sister Maria and told her to sell my apartment on the beach to help pay some of my medical expenses.

I still needed to find a roof over my head. My desire was to live in White Plains, but I ended up looking at a co-op in Port Chester. In the meantime, my furniture was floating again over the ocean, with my memories thrown into the wind. I was so alone, and still more misfortune was awaiting me.

After a long search, I finally found an apartment. I had some leftover money to use as a down payment. After I put the money down, I was not approved by the Board. I hired a lawyer to recuperate my money, but I lost most of it.

Crippled, with a cane, soon in a wheelchair, I fought the Board and was able to buy a different apartment, where I now live. I represented myself in front of the White Plains Court, sitting at my dining room table because I couldn't walk. I couldn't walk, but I answered every question. Even with my small stature, I would rise again like a skyscraper over the city. Once again, I never gave up and never abandoned that spirit to fight and to survive the storms of the world, with a broken heart and torn wings, but never without the hope for love and justice.

I walked with a cane from the pain, but my constant tears, calling my little sister's name, made me weaker and weaker. I missed my little sister, Maria, who protected me all the the time when I was a child.

One night, I became terribly sick in my new apartment. I started having chills and cold sweats, until I felt I was suffocating in my bed. I had the same symptoms as my sister Gabriella. I fell out of bed at midnight in a cold sweat. I was trembling from high fever and my forehead was ice cold. I felt dizzy and almost lost my sight. I felt my lungs in my throat. Somehow I was able to call an ambulance. When it arrived, it took forever for me to reach the door and open it. I felt that my lungs were collapsing. I started losing my mind, saying, "I am dying like my sister Gabriella! I am dying!" I ended up in the hospital with another serious case of pneumonia, lying in bed with intravenous antibiotics running through my veins. I was all alone and mentally devastated. Nobody was by my side.

After many months, I finally recovered from the attack of pneumonia, and was ready for the first hip operation. After the surgery, I felt keenly the pain of loneliness, struggling in the recovery process without my family. After six months of being crippled in a wheelchair, I went back to White Plains Hospital for the second hip operation. I was scared to face once again the challenges of life alone.

At 4:00 a.m. one cold morning, I slowly walked up the steps of the hospital, *avvolta in un calore artificiale della mia camicia da notte* (wrapped only in the artificial warmth of my nightgown). I held onto that sensation of warmth, imagining my mother's arms embracing me. But that warmth that I always dreamed about was not there to comfort me in the cold, empty hospital room. My tears wet my pale, sad face—the face of a woman who suffered all her life and for whom God still had no mercy.

My convalescence from the two operations lasted for three years. I had physical therapy. I walked with a cane. I cried mornings and nights, all by myself. While I was slowly recovering, I received a phone call from Adelina. She invited me to stay at her house for a week so that she could take care of me. One day, we decided to drive into town to do some shopping. I was just sitting down in the car, and hadn't pulled my legs all the way in, when Adelina suddenly started the car and backed up, dragging my legs along the driveway. I was screaming at the top of my lungs! Once again, I ended up in the emergency room.

The next day, I went back to my apartment in Port Chester.

At the beginning of my convalescence, I couldn't drive, so my nieces and my sister came to visit me. After a year, I was able to drive and I went as often as I could to visit my sister Adelina, until one day a tragic event happened.

Because she had diabetes, Adelina had been on dialysis for many years. One day, my niece Virginia called and told me that Adelina's dialysis hadn't gone well. She was ill and in the hospital. I decided to go to stay in Norwalk temporarily, to help my family. Cold December arrived, and I was going to the hospital every day to see Adelina. Here I was again, attending another sister at her deathbed. I needed to be strong for her, no matter how desperate and drained I felt. I fed my sister whenever I could, even though Virginia diligently sat at her mother's bedside each day to care for her.

On December 17th—Adelina's birthday—while I was holding my sister's right hand, Adelina passed away. I felt that my sister knew in her heart that I was there for her as she lay dying.

An ice storm developed on the same day that Adelina died. It was as though I were reliving the nightmare of my wedding, December 17th, 1961, when there'd been such a terrible blizzard. On the day of my sister's funeral, the church and the funeral parlor were nearly empty, because nobody could travel in the dreadful weather. Only the close family and a few friends were there. I felt an enormous pain in my broken heart and broken soul. Pain would never leave my life, and pain would remain my best companion.

I went back to my lonely life in my apartment, and to the tears of despair that I cried every day. To find some peace, I decided to listen to my doctor's advice. I started volunteering at Corpus Christi Church in Port Chester, twice a week. I find peace, happiness and joy helping the children at recess time at the Church. These children give me solace and fill my heart with joy with their pure beings.

I have finally found my childhood. As if I'd gone back in time, I often spend time around the church, the nuns and the innocent children once again. Each morning of my painful life, I wake up with new hope in my heart: just to hear the birds singing, just to look at the beautiful sunrise, just to say good morning to life, to each day. I take each moment, each day, as a gift to live life no matter what life itself throws at me. Maybe it is a new dress, the smile of a child, a rainbow in the sky, classical musical melodies in the air, that keep my spirit going and make me smile.

"Where am I going?" I ask myself.

Then I fly away in the form of a most beautiful monarch butterfly, with my fancy colorful wings, so royal and so vain in my beauty. I, a delicate butterfly, don't care that my wings are badly torn. These wings are the only ones I've ever had and the only ones God gave to me. I am brave, and with these torn wings, I fly away from my sorrow and pain towards the overarching sky and the lofty clouds.

Little Flower

One day, one hour, one moment.

*I hope that I will be with you where your heart is shaped like
a flower,*

with sparkling light that would touch me at night.

*As I follow that light on a cloudy day, I touch that flower,
and I have no more pain.*

*You are the flower with the sparkling light above the stars,
like a prayer around me, as I look for more each day.*

It is a gift that you gave to me.

That one day, one hour, one moment

*I will spend with you,
my little flower.*

CHAPTER FIFTEEN

Mamma, Mamma

A tribute to my mother and to all the mothers of the world.

All my life I have felt as if I were a child living under the loving wings of my Mamma. But then I was separated forever from her by the events of my painful life.

The love that my beautiful mother gave me during most of my life still lives inside of me. Her powerful love instilled in me the hope of being a mother myself and holding my baby in my arms, the way she held me as a child. I looked up at Mamma with the innocent eyes of a young girl and was inspired by her life and devotion to our family.

For this reason, I can't finish my book without writing these last words about my mother—my dear mother, Lucia—in my letter to her. With my poem I want to celebrate those mothers who love and cherish their children with all their hearts and souls.

Mamma, Mamma

You were singing a lullaby to me in the dark night.

I was waiting for you, pretending to sleep.

I heard your footsteps and then you kissed my forehead.

Your hair held the perfume of you, Mamma.

Your love nourished the heart of your lost and lonely little girl.

I was hoping again for your love. It was beautiful for me, Mamma.

Time doesn't erase the beauty of your face, with the veil of your sweet smile.

Painful but precious memories still live in me, even in my old age.

Your love is still alive in me.

These few words, that I give to you as a gift,

fly like the colorful flowers in our garden that are always in bloom, my dear Mamma.

CHAPTER SIXTEEN

Loreto Aprutino

*M*y *paese natale*—the town of my birth—is
Loreto Aprutino, an ancient town set in the hills of
the province of Pescara, above the Adriatic coast.
Loreto Aprutino, whose name was taken from the
abundant laurel trees that surrounded the town
during Roman times, has also been known throughout many centuries for its olive orchards and vineyards, producing the finest extra virgin olive oil and
prize-winning wines.

Among groves of pine and poplar trees, Loreto
Aprutino's gardens are always blossoming in its mild
climate. The town originally grew up around a medieval castle, first built in the ninth century. Restored
by the Chiola family in the nineteenth century, the
magnificent Castello Chiola now stands on the site
of the original castle. Nearby is the Church of St.
Peter the Apostle, dating from the eleventh century.
Its tall *campanile* (bell tower) stands above the town,

sending the sounds of its bells into the distance.

I still see in my mind those giant poplar trees that grew over the porticos of the ancient buildings, under the shadow of the colorful houses, with their wrought-iron balconies. In the fresh air of the morning, the neighbors chatted with their doors and windows open, feeling in the breeze droplets from the fountains in the village, with their dancing waters in the pure air.

As a little girl, I woke up each morning to that fresh and fragrant air. I walked with my backpack on my shoulders, along the winding streets filled with tall, perfumed pine trees, on my way to school at the Convento del Gesù (Convent of Jesus). In the narrow streets, the little houses, faded and discolored by centuries, huddled next to each other, their sides touching, resembling *merletto ricamato* (embroidered lace). I climbed up the steep streets to the convent, which looked like a tall castle from above, with its foundations lost in the shadows of the trees.

Just outside the town is the medieval church of Santa Maria in Piano, which is decorated inside with beautiful frescoes showing the lives of the saints. Also dating from the Renaissance is the famous painting, *Giudizio particolare delle anime* (Unusual punishment of souls), which depicts scenes from the Last Judgement.

Of the many traditions in my town, the most famous and unusual is the Festa di San Zopito—the Feast of St. Zopito, the patron saint of Loreto Aprutino. Every spring, on the first Monday after Pentecost, all the balconies are festooned with colors, and the streets are decorated with colorful *ricami smerlati* (scalloped embroidery) on the dresses of the women gathered around. Tourists arrive from the nearby towns to witness this unique tradition.

On the Feast of St. Zopito, a big white ox dressed in a festive outfit processes through the streets to the cathedral. The ox wears on its head a tall *pettinata* (comb) hung with colorful ribbons and little bells. Riding on the ox's back is a small boy dressed in white, holding a little hand-painted white umbrella over his head and carrying a red rose in his teeth. The ox and the boy are accompanied by bagpipers, and followed by men on horseback, representing the *vetturali*, tradesmen who used to travel from village to village carrying virgin olive oil to sell.

After winding through the town, the procession, along with the ox, enters the cathedral. At the altar, the ox kneels to show its devotion, as the people pray during the Mass. Only when the Mass is over does the ox rise again to stand on all four legs.

I will hold these memories of my dear birthplace in my mind and heart forever: Loreto

Aprutino, in the foothills of the magestic mountains of Gran Sasso.

Chapter Without End

Life blocked with iron gates, over the world's limits
I was flying
to find myself consumed by time.

I stopped for a moment, for a breath of air under the open
sky.
Lovely pause, a light in the night was singing springtime,
with the lovely wind in my hair.

I was looking at the immensity of the sea, a thousand lights
of clear light,
to satisfy my heart, my desire for love.

While I was still dreaming,
along the roads with trees all around, I was hiding
from the the rain of summertime,
from the grey morning.
I was turning and I was looking at you.

At the sound of the bells, a thousand sparks of light,
you were singing mom's heart, with an echo to the sky,
while you were hugging me tight to your heart.

In my life path, with pain for love, I was following the
curved roads depicted on illustrated postcards,
with uneven pathways, blossomed a little flower.

To follow the golden fireflies, I touched the highest waves of the mountain.

To relive the hours of life, like a bud, the scent of you,
Mamma,
that will never die, because you are real, Mamma.
You are mine, on the right path of hope.

Life is love. It is a garden—
the same one you cultivated with your love,
the garden you decorated only with roses.

Giovanna's Garden

Life will continue to touch the sea and the sky, that will never die.

As life goes on, the illustrated postcard will come alive

where the children are growing,

and the wind will blow the seed to the next garden

where the flower blooms, perfuming the air,

The heartbeat under the starry night

Where all of us caress the moment for evermore.

I know that life is worth living.

As I live my life, I know that tomorrow will be a better day.

As I look up at the dark night, I see the moon light up the sky

To satisfy the lovers' desire!

Because love is real and life is beautiful,

And that's why my book will continue on for the next generation.

Be happy and smile!

You will see the garden cultivated with roses,

And those thorns will never prick you.

About the Author

Giovanna Maria Acciavatti grew up in the Abruzzo region of Italy, near the Adriatic Sea. She came to the United States as a young woman, and has made her home here ever since. She now lives in Port Chester, New York.

Born into a family of talented designers, she owned and ran her own fur design boutique in Bronxville, New York for many years. In recent years, she has been writing poetry in both Italian and English. This is her first book.